Shakespeare's Cues and Prompts

Continuum Shakespeare Studies

Shakespeare in Japan – Tetsuo Kishi and Graham Bradshaw
Shakespeare in China – Murray J. Levith

Shakespeare's Cues and Prompts

MURRAY J. LEVITH

continuum

Continuum International Publishing Group

The Tower Building   80 Maiden Lane
11 York Road   Suite 704
London SE1 7NX   New York NY 10038

British Library Cataloguing-in-Publication Data
A catalogue record for this book is available from the British Library.

ISBN: HB: 0-8264-9597-4
      9780826495976

Library of Congress Cataloging-in-Publication Data
A catalog record for this book is available from the Library of Congress.

Typeset by Fakenham Photosetting Limited, Fakenham, Norfolk NR21 8NN
Printed and bound in Great Britain by Cromwell Press Ltd, Trowbridge, Wiltshire

As always, for Tina

Immature poets imitate; mature poets steal; bad poets deface what they take, and good poets make it into something better, or at least something different. The good poet welds his theft into a whole of feeling which is unique, utterly different from that from which it was torn; the bad poet throws it into something which has no cohesion.

T. S. Eliot, from *The Sacred Wood: Essays on Poetry and Criticism.* New York: University Paperbacks, 1960, p. 125.

Contents

Acknowledgments

Several of the chapters in this study evolved from seminar papers prepared for recent Shakespeare Association of America meetings. Two of the seminars were focused on Shakespeare's sources and another on King James I. These topics stimulated my further interest in issues and questions that I was already thinking about, and prodded me to refine my thoughts in preliminary essays. For organizing these sessions I should like to thank the seminar leaders: Professors Catherine Loomis, David M. Bergeron, Lori Humphrey Newcomb, and Dr. Barbara A. Mowat of the Folger Shakespeare Library. Acknowledgment is also due the other seminar participants for their helpful criticisms and suggestions concerning my work. One of my papers developed into a finished article, '*Coriolanus* and *The Flaying of Marsyas*'; for permission to reprint a revised version of it as part of Chapter 3, thanks to the Edwin Mellen Press, *Shakespeare Yearbook 2000, Volume 11: Shakespeare and the Visual Arts*, Holger Klein and James L. Harner, editors. Again a 'thank you' to Barbara Mowat, who had kind comments about my paper on *A Midsummer Night's Dream*, despite the fact that by seminar time I had not discovered her perceptive and closely related article. Professors Barbara L. Parker and Terri Bourus, too, complimented my paper on King James as Iago, and gave me the confidence to expand my rather bold argument. Professor Peter Holland read a later version of this essay, prompting me to tighten it further. I thank each of them for their welcome comments. Professor John W. Mahon and Ellen Macleod Mahon published my essay 'Shakespeare's *Merchant* and Marlowe's Other Play' in *The Merchant of Venice: New Critical Essays* (New York: Routledge, 2002), and I use it here in a lightly revised version with their permission as a part of my Chapter 2. John Mahon and Thomas A. Pendleton, co-editors of *The Shakespeare Newsletter*, published a version of '*Richard III*: The Dragon and Saint George' (53:2 [Summer 2003]), and I use that with permission as well.

Art Resource, NY, granted permission for reproducing the images designated as Figures 1, 2 and 3: Rembrandt's *Faust in his Study, Watching a Magic Disc*, Titian's *The Flaying of Marsyas*, and Giulio Romano's *The Flaying of Marsyas*. The Yale University Art Gallery granted permission for reproducing Figure 4: Giulio Romano's

Gaius Marcius Coriolanus Discovered Among the Volscians. The Folger Shakespeare Library granted permission for reproducing Figure 5: *St. George and the Dragon*. Further credits are given beneath each illustration.

Skidmore College's Lucy Scribner Library and its professional staff have been an enormous help throughout this project, and I would like to thank especially College Librarian Ruth S. Copans, Access Services Librarian John A. Cosgrove, Interlibrary Loan Supervisor Amy B. Syrell and recently retired Marilyn Sheffer for their ongoing help. Last but not least, the many students in my Shakespeare courses over the last several years have not only challenged my interpretations and analyses but, indeed, contributed more than a little to them. I thank them for their enthusiasm, excitement, and insights.

Chapter 1
Shakespeare, intertextuality and sources

Shakespeare, like Bottom in *A Midsummer Night's Dream*, is a weaver. The playwright's 'web of ... mingled yarn' is the linsey-woolsey of his explicit and implicit narrative and dramatic sources, historical and cultural prompts, and other multifaceted intertexts woven into the fabric of his comedies, tragedies and histories.[1] Julia Kristeva's term *intertextuality*, from the Latin *intertexto* for 'intermingle while weaving,' suggests that a Shakespeare work, as any other, 'builds itself as a mosaic of quotations, every text is absorption and transformation of another text.'[2] Roland Barthes, continuing the metaphor, agrees that a given 'text is a tissue, a woven fabric.'[3] Thus, to interpret a Shakespeare play, 'to discover its meaning, or meanings,' according to Graham Allen, 'is to trace those [intertextual] relations, ... a process of moving between texts.'[4] This study highlights some examples of largely unrecognized and sometimes subtle strands of Shakespeare's intertextual tapestries in selected plays. Such intertexts represent mostly conscious and adapted sources that once noticed may help contribute to fresh understandings of the plays examined.

Kristeva's concept of intertextuality, however, is not really about fixed influences, but rather posits a far-reaching complex of imbedded ideologies, sociologies and cultural nuances and complexities. Along these lines, Stephen Lynch writes that 'Shakespeare's plays are ... now seen as interventions in preexistent fields of textuality. The old notion of particular and distinct sources has given way to new notions of boundless and heterogeneous textuality.'[5] Poststructuralist theory also holds that even the idea of Shakespeare as 'author' is to be questioned – and not, to be sure, in the anti-Stratfordian sense. Barthes asserts the 'Death of the Author,' claiming that the writer's 'only power is to mix writings' and that a language 'scriptor' (his term) speaks in any work (145–47). Barthes counters what he calls the 'myth of filiation'; that is, author as textual 'parent.' His idea seems especially relevant for early-English drama, where playwrights mostly collaborated not only in the writing of plays but also in contributing variously to them as theater company actors, producers and shareholders. Stephen Orgel, for one, claims that 'Actors are the original poststructuralists, assuming throughout the history of theater, that the author does not control the play, the interpreter does; and that, indeed, there is, for the purposes of performance – which are, after all, the purposes of drama – no author, only an infinitely mutable script.[6] Michel Foucault, too, contends, in a celebrated essay, that the traditional concept of 'author' is anachronistic.[7]

Barthes distinguishes, as does Kristeva, between sources or influences and intertextuality. He writes, 'The intertextual in which every text is held, it itself being the text-between of another text, is not to be confused with some origin of the text: to try to find the "sources", the "influences" of a work, is to fall in with the myth of filiation' (160). Shakespeare thus would be diminished to a revisionary mediator of inherited texts, cultural constructs and other multi-faceted cues and prompts rather than an autonomous playwright and artist.

But granted that Shakespeare is a 'scriptor,' is he also more than this as understood in his moment – that is, mostly a unique and solitary 'author' to be acknowledged as such? His name began appearing together with his plays beginning March 10, 1598, with the publication of *A Pleasant Conceited Comedie called Loues labors lost*. It continued thereafter, first with newly issued versions of the formerly anonymous quartos of *Richard II* and *Richard III*, and then other publications presumably as a selling point. Peter Ackroyd argues,

> The publication of *Love's Labour's Lost* can be seen … as a highly significant event in the creation of the modern conception of the writer. It was not the least of Shakespeare's accomplishments to elevate, and perhaps even to create, the status and the reputation of the commercial author. … The author may have come out of the printing press rather than the theatre, as this narrative suggests, but the literary and cultural identity of the writer could no longer be ignored.[8]

Shakespeare was on the cusp of a significant shift in the print culture of drama, suggested further in the year of his death by Ben Jonson's *Works* (1616) and his own posthumous *First Folio* (1623). Orgel, for example, contends that Ben Jonson, dissatisfied with the fluid, theatrical versions of his plays, 'took control' of them by asserting his 'authority' when he 'rewrote' them for publication (2). When Jonson published *Every Man Out of His Humour* he declared himself 'author' on the title page.[9] Similarly, when John Heminges and Henry Condell put together the handsome folio volume of Shakespeare's collected plays, claiming to preserve 'the True Originall Copies,' they cited Shakespeare specifically as 'Author' in their prefatory 'To the great Variety of Readers': 'It had bene a thing, we confesse, worthie to haue bene wished, that the Author himselfe had liu'd to haue set forth, and ouerseen his owne writings.' Jonson's celebratory poem as well is inscribed (with the word 'author' in caps no less), 'To the memory of my belloued, The AVTHOR Mr. William Shakespeare,' and 'Authour' is also the word used in the heading of other dedicatory poems. It is clear that his own age came to view Shakespeare as a discrete 'author.'

The 'author' designation gives authority to the presumed primary 'creator' of dramatic texts, even, in Shakespeare's case, folio texts not 'ouerseen' by the playwright himself. Since an acting company commissioned plays and perhaps even determined their subjects, farming out the writing to one or more of the company's playwrights, with actors revising the scripts along the way to and in performance, an early-English play was typically not a one-person creative act. It was most often a collaborative effort, continuously subject to revision and change. Philip Henslowe's diaries reveal that only thirty-four of the eighty-nine plays he supervised at the Swan were written by a single author and the other fifty-five collaborative efforts (Ackroyd 331). Despite the fact that Shakespeare was playwright, actor and shareholder in his company, and thus he was probably in on much of the collaboration, Orgel contends, what we now label 'Shakespeare' is nonetheless surely 'contaminated and indeed determined by a myriad of other texts' (35).

Harold Bloom, in *The Anxiety of Influence* (and other books), challenges the vast plurality and disappearance of the autonomous author celebrated by Kristeva, Barthes and their followers.[10] Bloom denies largely unbounded intertextual fields for literature, asserting that only other *literary* texts are relevant – works, that is, struggle with and against their predecessors. Furthermore, a text under scrutiny, according to Bloom, itself often directs one to the appropriate intertext(s).[11] Bloom, however, pointedly omits Shakespeare from his 'anxiety of influence' discussion:

> The greatest poet in our language is excluded ... for several reasons. One is necessarily historical: Shakespeare belongs to the giant age before the flood, before the anxiety of influence became central to poetic consciousness. Another has to do with the contrast between dramatic

and lyric form. ... The main cause, though, is that Shakespeare's prime precursor was Marlowe, a poet very much smaller that his inheritor. ... Shakespeare is the largest instance in the language of ... the absolute absorption of the precursor. (11)

In another place, Bloom writes, 'Marlowe was swallowed up by Shakespeare, as a minnow by a whale, though Marlowe had strong enough aftertaste to compel Shakespeare to some wry innuendos.'[12] Indeed, he did, as we shall see, in the chapter that follows. Ackroyd, too, notes that 'Only Shakespeare [of the Elizabethan dramatists] ... seems to have quoted so extensively from his rival Marlowe' (161).

It is apparent that most, if not all, of Shakespeare's plays, at least in part, relate to specific and discoverable antecedent materials, and thus a source type of 'intertext.' Geoffrey Bullough's monumental work and Kenneth Muir's *Sources of Shakespeare's Plays* continue to be indispensable for locating Shakespeare's clear and likely cues and prompts.[13] More recent studies concerning influences include, among others, Robert S. Miola's *Shakespeare's Reading*, Leonard Barkan's 'What did Shakespeare Read?,' and Stuart Gillespie's *Shakespeare's Books: A Dictionary of Shakespeare's Sources.*[14] Jack J. Jorgens employs a happy image to explain how sources illuminate a text: 'In a source study one peers over the shoulder of the artist and watches the way he works with his raw materials. The earlier work clarifies, enriches and provides a lever for discussion of the later.'[15]

Throughout his career Shakespeare adapted sometimes canonical but mostly contemporary works in English as well as in several other languages. Michael Wood aptly labels the playwright 'a derivative writer in the best sense, usually borrowing and adapting an existing plot and always going after the inherited ... with a great feel for the basics of storytelling.'[16] Lifting plots and language in Shakespeare's time was not considered plagiarism; rather, it was considered an important part of artistic and dramatic creativity. Shakespeare's specific pre-texts range from the closely followed Thomas Lodge's *Rosalynde* or the Moor's story from Giraldi Cinthio's *Hecatommithi*, both of which he reworked and complicated as he rewrote (see Lynch); to a variety of prompts for *Love's Labor's Lost*, *A Midsummer Night's Dream*, *The Merry Wives of Windsor* and *The Tempest*; to favorite sourcebooks that include Ovid's *Metamorphoses*, Thomas North's *Plutarch* and Raphael Holinshed's *Chronicles*. Shakespeare also used what was in his contemporary air; he knew his audience's prejudices and beliefs, and thus in his plays could recast to popular tastes source history, politics, cultural myths and narratives. Lynch notes, the playwright's theater 'drew ... audiences that by modern standards would be considered virtually monocultural' (116). These audiences were composed mostly of people who had enough leisure to attend afternoon performances, with the gentry and the lower classes mixing. Indeed, as one elitist put it, 'at our common plays and such like exercises which be commonly exposed to be seen for money, every lewd person thinks himself (for his penny) worthy of the chief and most commodious place.'[17] Shakespeare set about to please all, whether they were courtly aristocrats or common folk.

* * * *

The present volume examines a number of *types* of Shakespearean intertextual prompts imbedded in and/or cuing selected works: an unrecognized dramatic source from a contemporary play, images likely remembered from a favorite Latin classic, a quasi-mythic narrative, a prompt involving a familiar British national myth and an item of contemporary political interest.

Christopher Marlowe's *The Tragical History of Doctor Faustus*, as we shall see, clearly informs a reading of Shakespeare's *The Merchant of Venice*. *Doctor Faustus*, together with one of its own sources, the *English Faust Book*, has been overlooked as a crucial prompt for *The Merchant of Venice*, perhaps because of the attention paid to its more obvious cousin, Marlowe's *The Jew of Malta*. Yet it is clear that Shakespeare weaves the Faust story deliberately and unmistakably into the fabric of his Venetian comedy.

The next example examines images Shakespeare likely recalled from narratives in Golding's translation of Ovid's *Metamorphoses*, used in his late tragedy *Coriolanus* and his earlier comedy *The Merry Wives of Windsor*. The playwright's brief description of the bloody warrior Caius Martius emerging from the walls of the conquered Corioli (1.6.21–22) hearkens back to a similar arresting and bloody image from a seemingly unrelated narrative in Ovid. While the satyr Marsyas' story at first seems to have little to do with Shakespeare's *Coriolanus*, there is, in fact, an intriguing web of associations, some of them thematic and others involving a Titian painting and its antecedents, which ties in with the tragedy in an interesting and meaningful way. Similarly, some scholars recognize the Actaeon myth as a correlative for the Herne the Hunter episode toward the end of *The Merry Wives of Windsor*.

Chapter 4 concerns *A Midsummer Night's Dream*. This early comedy is truly a weave of intertextual sources, but is shown to be significantly informed overall by the Theseus legend that brings together Shakespeare's various plot elements and groups of characters. What Shakespeare includes from the legend, as well as what he leaves out but implies, neatly ties together and unifies his comedy.

A further example of a type of intertextuality is Shakespeare's use of the English national myth of Saint George and the Dragon that forms a backdrop for *Richard III*. The patron saint's hagiography, together with its related topology, serves as a self-conscious analogue for plot and meaning in this history play. Here Shakespeare sets about mostly to tell the dragon's story. His cues range from Edmund Spenser's *The Faerie Queene* to the Guy of Warwick legend, local for Shakespeare.

While contemporary Tudor 'propaganda' is the focus in *Richard III*, anti-Stuart political commentary is to be found in *Othello*. As James Shapiro notes, 'Shakespeare was a dramatist alert to the factional world of contemporary politics' (17). The playwright argues by way of his character Iago that Queen Elizabeth's heir to the throne should not be James VI of Scotland. The tragedy *Othello* is thus freshly seen as a part of the clandestine discussion of the complicated and confused succession issue, forced underground by Elizabeth herself.

The concluding chapter of this study highlights some of Shakespeare's own early works as cues and prompts for his later plays. After looking at some brief examples of what Shakespeare recycles, I analyze the considerable debt the problem comedy *All's Well That Ends Well* owes to the early comedy *The Taming of the Shrew*. Both are coming-of-age stories with an education theme, one with a male learner and the other with a female.

Chapter 2
Shakespeare's Merchant *and* Marlowe's other play

Launcelot Gobbo's confused but colorful monologue in *The Merchant of Venice* (2.2.1–32) is an important clue to the dynamics of Shakespeare's Faustian comedy. We recall that the clown is contemplating breaking his servile bond with the Jew Shylock, 'the very devil incarnation,' in order to cast his lot with the Christian Bassanio, who has 'the grace of God' (2.2.150–51). Launcelot imagines himself at the center of a morality struggle, a Faust character with a good angel, his 'conscience,' at one elbow and a bad angel, the 'fiend,' at the other. Of course, he gets things comically confused, but ultimately decides to 'run' from the Jew.

Christopher Marlowe's *Doctor Faustus* and Shakespeare's *The Merchant of Venice* were written within a few years of each other. Although the precise dates of their composition are not known, *Doctor Faustus* was likely written in 1593, the year of Marlowe's death, and *The Merchant of Venice* in 1596–97.[1] Moreover, *Doctor Faustus* was acted twenty-plus times between late September or early October of 1594 and January 5, 1597;[2] that is, it was on the boards during the very time Shakespeare was writing his *Merchant*.

It is clear that *The Merchant of Venice* not only owes something to Marlowe's usually acknowledged *The Jew of Malta*,[3] but also, and importantly, to his Faust play as well. The plot details are different, but the ideational structure is recognizably similar. In both plays, for example, there is a singular bond with a devil-associated character, a central 'Faust' protagonist to be tested, 'correct' and 'incorrect' character choices, and specific place settings associated with 'good' and 'bad' values. Further, both plays can be seen as about the nature of the good Christian life in the face of worldly temptations. Peter Ackroyd notes, that Shakespeare 'was mightily impressed and influenced by Marlowe is not in doubt; it is also clear that in his earliest plays Shakespeare stole or copied some of his lines, parodied him, and generally competed with him.'[4] And, as T.S. Eliot avers in his 1919 essay on Marlowe, 'when Shakespeare borrowed from him, which was pretty often at the beginning, Shakespeare either made something inferior or something different.'[5] In the case of *The Merchant of Venice*, it was nothing 'inferior.'

Marlowe's main source for *Doctor Faustus* is the so-called *English Faust Book 'The History of the Damnable Life and Deserved Death of Doctor John Faustus'* (1592), translated by one P.F. Gent. from the German *Historia von D. Johan Fausten* (1587).[6] Shakespeare's *Merchant* may owe something to this *English Faust Book* as well. In it there is an episode about a Jew that is conflated in Marlowe's *Doctor Faustus* with the 'Horse-courser' episode (4.5–6). The *Faust Book* chapter is titled 'How Doctor Faustus borrowed money of a Jew and laid his own leg to pawn for it' (Chapter 33). The tale begins with Faustus' 'merry jest to deceive a Jew,' echoing Shylock's 'merry bond' (1.3.173) to deceive Antonio.[7] The magician borrows 'threescore dollars,' similar to the 'three thousand ducats' in Shakespeare's play. As surety for the Jew, Faustus 'cuts off' his leg, his 'pawn of flesh,' to be reclaimed and sewn back upon repayment of the loan. 'Thinking it would stink and so infect my house,' the Jew discards the severed limb; besides, he says, 'it is too hard a piece of work to set it on again' (Jones 153). Of course, the loan is repaid in time and Faustus demands his leg or, if the Jew cannot produce it, the Jew's own limb![8] As in *The Merchant*, the *Faust Book* Jew is tricked, defeated and made to look foolish. After pleading to save his leg, he is forced to pay additional money beyond the loan to satisfy the magician.

The Merchant of Venice, like *Doctor Faustus*, is a play about choice.[9] The words 'choice,' 'choose,' 'chooses,' 'chooseth,' 'choosing,' 'chose' and 'chosen' occur more than fifty times in Shakespeare's play. We have already noted that Launcelot Gobbo chooses to leave the Jew's service. So too does Jessica leave her father's house, to elope with Lorenzo and 'Become a Christian' (2.3.21). The presumably Muslim Morocco and the surely Catholic Arragon cannot choose the proper casket and so win Portia because they are dazzled by external show and egotistical pride, rather than understanding the Christian message that least is most and 'All that glisters is not gold' (2.7.65). Additionally, as Barbara Lewalski argues, 'the defeat and lessoning of Morocco and Aragon [*sic*] foreshadows the defeat and conversion of Shylock, for he represents in somewhat different guise these same antichristian values of worldliness and self-righteousness.'[10] The three alien characters are without mates at the end, doomed to the sterile life their world-views suggest.[11] Indeed, Arragon reminds the audience of the consequences of an improper choice in the lottery: 'I am enjoin'd by oath ... never in my life / To woo a maid in way of marriage' (2.9.9–13). So too does

Portia remind Morocco: 'You must take your chance, / And either not attempt to choose at all, / Or swear before you choose, if you choose wrong / Never to speak to lady afterward / In way of marriage' (2.1.38–42).[12]

On the other hand, Bassanio, when given a choice to make, chooses correctly: the humble leaden casket that nonetheless promises a golden future of love and marriage. He comments, 'The world is still deceiv'd with ornament' (3.2.74), a slur at those we have seen choose before him. Lewalski contends, 'At the allegorical level, the caskets signify everyman's choice of the paths to spiritual life or death' (336). Thus, the selection of the leaden casket by Bassanio is understood as life-affirming. As Jessica notes, 'For having such a blessing in his lady, / He finds the joys of heaven here on earth' (3.5.75–76). The lover's name comes from *basanite*, the touchstone used to test for true gold.[13] Bassanio seems intuitively to understand not only which casket to choose, but also the difference between the letter and spirit of a bond: when he is faced with surrendering his wedding ring, he again makes the appropriate Christian choice.

Despite Lancelot's 'good angel/bad angel' monologue and Bassanio's proper choices, Antonio is clearly the central Faustian character in *The Merchant of Venice*. However, Antonio differs significantly from Marlowe's magician. Whereas Doctor Faustus signs over his eternal *soul* to the devil, Antonio secures his loan from the vengeful Shylock pledging only 'an equal pound / Of … fair *flesh*' from his *body* (1.3.149–50; emphasis mine). As the devil Mephistopheles concedes in Marlowe's play, the body 'is but little worth' (5.1.86). The magician, when sealing his bond, has clear warnings that he is doing something damnable: his blood only 'trickles' from his arm and then 'congeals' (2.1.57, 62), so that fire must be brought to liquify it. Signing the 'bill' turns out to be a laborious process, also underlining its tragic seriousness. 'What might the staying of my blood portend?' Doctor Faustus asks rhetorically (2.1.65). Conversely, and despite Bassanio's repeated misgivings – 'You shall not seal to such a bond for me, / I'll rather dwell in my necessity,' or 'I like not fair terms and a villain's mind' (1.3.154–55,179) – Antonio readily agrees to Shylock's not-so-'merry bond.' The magician signs over his soul for self-serving knowledge, worldly power and fame, while Antonio pledges his pound of flesh only to help his good friend. The merchant thus suggests the New Testament teaching: 'Greater loue then this hathe no man, when any man bestoweth his life for his friends' (John 15.13).[14]

At the beginning of their plays both the magician and the merchant are unhappy. Doctor Faustus, though, thinks he understands the cause of his disquiet. Although favored with deep learning, he is frustrated by human limitations and thus seeks to go beyond what he has and knows. What 'Faustus most desires ... [is] a world of profit and delight, / Of power, of honor, of omnipotence' (1.1.50-52). Such earthly rewards seem at first grand and worth a hellish contract, but ultimately they are shown to be small payment in exchange for eternal damnation after a mere twenty-four years.[15] Moreover, many of the things the magician desires he does not get: a wife, straight answers to important questions (e.g. 'who made the world?' [2.2.71–72]) and so on. What he does receive are various diversions, including the lavish masque of the Seven Deadly Sins. These entertainments, to be sure, are fleeting and are meant to shift attention away from his fearsome bargain with Lucifer.

The magician, most of all, would have the power of God or Jesus Christ. At the beginning of his play he complains, 'thou are still but Faustus and a man. / Coulds't thou make men to live eternally / Or being dead raise them to life again / Then this profession [i.e. philosophy] were to be esteemed' (1.1.21–24). While Antonio cannot raise the dead, his willingness to place his corporeal body in bond for love of his fellow man aligns him with Christ. Antonio demonstrates Christ-like patience in the face of threat from the devil-associated character Shylock who harrows him: 'I do oppose / My patience to his fury, and am arm'd / To suffer, with a quietness of spirit, / The very tyranny and rage of his' (4.1.10–13). Lewalski observes, 'Antonio baring his breast to shed his blood for the debt of another, [makes plain] ... the identification with Christ' (339). Just as Doctor Faustus' devilish bond must be signed in blood, Antonio's would-be sacrifice for love is also a potential blood rite. Antonio is, again in Lewalski's words, 'a perfect embodiment of Christian love' (331).

Antonio's melancholy at the start of *The Merchant of Venice* is something that he himself does not understand: 'In sooth, I know not why I am so sad' (1.1.1). He is neither in love with a woman nor overly worried about his ships. Yet his merchant's life in commercial Venice and his obvious wealth do not give him fulfillment and ease. Unlike Marlowe's overweening magician, however, Antonio senses that his true 'estate' is not *this world* or *this life*. He explains, 'My ventures are not in one bottom trusted, / Nor to one place; nor is my whole estate / Upon the fortune of this present year' (1.1.42–44). He seems aware of a promised future. Antonio goes on to say that because the world is transitory, 'I hold the world *but as the world*' (I.1.77; emphasis mine). His words recall Matthew 6.19–20: 'Lay not up treasures for your selves upon the earth, where the mothe & canker corrupt, & where theves digge through, and steale. But lay up treasures for your selves in heaven.' The merchant is willing, therefore, to pledge his earthly body as a Christian saint might do. Cynthia Lewis contends that 'the very name *Antonio*,' with its saintly associations, 'suggested to audiences of high English Renaissance drama a willingness to compromise one's own well being for a person or principle seen as more important – or higher – than the self' (45).[16]

Like Antonio, Portia is melancholy too. The reason for her weariness 'of this great world' (1.2.2) is that she is denied choice of a husband. Portia complains, 'O me, the word choose! I may neither choose who I would, nor refuse who I dislike; so is the will of a living daughter curb'd by the will of a dead father: ... I cannot choose one, nor refuse none' (1.2.22–26). She later adds, 'In terms of choice I am not solely led / By nice direction of a maiden's eyes; / ... the lott'ry of my destiny / Bars me the right of voluntary choosing' (2.1.13–16). Portia has no choice because she functions in part as the allegorical 'portion' (as in her name), the symbolic prize her heavenly father offers as reward to the Christian Everyman. In Shakespeare's allegory, Portia is a kind of Fairy Queen or Queen Elizabeth, presiding over a special and clearly otherworldly place. Belmont is a 'beautiful mountain,' as its name suggests. It can be seen as fairyland England, much in the manner of Edmund Spenser's *The Faerie Queene*, another text from the 1590s. Like Queen Elizabeth herself, Portia rejects various inappropriate suitors despite their pedigrees. Identified with the True Church, she will wed only the true-born English Everyman, represented by Bassanio. The lover is like Prince Arthur who is to be united ultimately with the Fairy Queen and all she represents. She offers the prospect of salvation through spiritual love and marriage to the True – that is, Anglican – Church, and so contrasts with Marlowe's Helen.

Doctor Faustus at first asks Mephistopheles for a wife, but when confronted with a woman devil, a 'hot whore' (2.1.152), he changes his mind. Mephistopheles agrees: 'Marriage is but a ceremonial toy' (2.1.153). However, late in Marlowe's play Faustus demands that Helen appear, 'To glut the longing of my heart's desire' (5.1.88). But Helen does not have the power to make the magician 'immortal with a kiss'; indeed, the woman whose 'face ... launched a thousand ships' to war has 'lips [that] suck forth [Faustus'] soul' (5.1.96, 99).

'Helen,' in Jan Kott's view, is the 'sign and omen of doom,'[17] just as Portia represents fulfillment in Shakespeare's play.

Portia is also, just as Antonio, a Christ-like figure. She obeys her father's will, and rescues the merchant, a would-be Christian martyr. When Bassanio is ready to choose from among the caskets she affirms, 'I stand for sacrifice' (3.2.57). Her statement sharply contrasts with Shylock's, 'I stand for judgment' (4.1.103) or 'I stand here for law' (4.1.142), later in the trial scene. Coming down from heavenly Belmont to earthly Venice, she assumes the role of Balthazar (a name associated with one of the three Magi [see Matthew 2]), arguing eloquently that mercy is necessary for sinful man, as against Shylock's prideful Hebrew notion of self-righteousness. Her text comes from John's First Epistle (8): 'If we say that we have no sinne, we deceive our selves, and trueth is not in us,' a passage quoted by Doctor Faustus in his very first speech.

Shylock has made Doctor Faustus' selfish choice of the superficial temporal world before Shakespeare's play begins. G.K. Hunter cites the tradition of 'seeing Jewishness as a moral condition, the climactic "Jewish choice" being that which rejected Christ and chose Barabbas, rejected the Saviour and chose the robber, rejected the spirit and chose the flesh, rejected the treasure that is in heaven and chose the treasure that is on earth.'[18] Shylock is concerned with profit, ducats and revenge. The Jew despises the merchant because he is a Christian, and also for lending 'out money gratis' (1.3.44). Shylock has aligned himself with the 'bad angel' or devil character in Shakespeare's Faustian comedy. When asked why he wants Antonio's pound of flesh he replies, 'To bait fish withal' (3.1.53). Perhaps his meaning is: to catch other Christians 'upon the hip' (1.3.46). If Jesus would be a fisher of men to save them, Shylock would fish to ensnare. Marlowe's magician asks Mephistopheles, 'What good will my soul do thy lord [Lucifer]?' (2.1.40), and the devil replies, 'Enlarge his kingdom' (2.1.41).

The Jew is associated explicitly with the devil many times in *Merchant*, and Jessica describes their 'house' as 'hell' (2.3.2). The biblical allusion is to John (8.44), where Jesus chides the doubting Jews: 'Ye are of your father the devil.' Like the devil, Shylock 'can cite Scripture for his purpose. / [He is] An evil soul producing holy witness' (1.3.98–99). He gives a twisted reading of the Jacob and Laban's sheep story (see Genesis 30.31–43) as a way of justifying his usury, and perhaps his exegesis is meant to satirize Hebrew midrashic interpretation. Bassanio remarks, 'In religion, / What damned error, but some sober brow / Will bless it, and approve it with a text, /

Hiding the grossness with fair ornament?' (3.2.77–80). The devil is a Jew because, as Kott affirms, 'The devil always appears in disguise; ... otherwise he could frighten but not tempt' (6).

Shylock's hellish world is without harmony, vengeful, grimly austere, humorless. The Jew tells his daughter, 'Let not the sound of shallow fopp'ry enter / My sober house' (2.5.35–36); he orders, 'Lock up my doors, and when you hear the drum / And the vile squealing of the wry-neck'd fife, / Clamber not you up to the casements then, / ... But stop my house's ears' (2.5.29–34). Shylock has no time for masques and music. However, as Lorenzo reminds us, 'The man that hath no music in himself, ... / Is fit for treasons, stratagems, and spoils; / ... his affections dark as [Erebus] [i.e. hell]: / Let no such man be trusted' (5.1.83–88). When Shylock is 'bid forth to supper' by Antonio and his fellows, he goes 'in hate, to feed upon / The prodigal Christian' (2.5.11, 14–15); that is, to 'spend' or waste their generous offer of food and hospitality. The Jew is hateful and his focus is on revenge and ducats. Lewalski contends, 'This concern for the world poisons all his relations with others, and even his love for Jessica' (330). Shylock's comment about his only child who has run away is chilling: 'I would my daughter were dead at my foot, and the jewels in her ear! Would she were hears'd at my foot, and the ducats in her coffin!' (3.1.87–90).

Venice, the title setting for *Merchant*, is among the places Doctor Faustus visits during his travels. The magician describes the city's cathedral as 'a sumptuous temple ... / That threats the stars with her aspiring top, / Whose frame is pav'd with sundry colour'd stones / And roof'd aloft with curious work in gold' (3.1.17–20). This description of Saint Mark's is in the tradition of Spenser's view of Saint Peter's in Rome, which the poet sees as a 'House of Pride' (*The Faerie Queene* 1.4.4), and was common contemporary Protestant cant against the perceived wealth, extravagance and ostentation of the Catholic Church. The Revels' editor of Marlowe's play points out that Saint Mark's does not have (and never did have) an 'aspiring top.'[19]

Protestant schoolmaster Roger Ascham reported that he witnessed more sin in nine days in Venice than he saw in nine years in London.[20] After his brief visit, the queen's tutor describes Venice as home to the '*diabolo incarnato*,' the 'Englishman Italianated':

He, that by living, and traveling in *Italie*, bringeth home into England out of *Italie*, the Religion, the learning, the policie, the experience, the maners of *Italie*. That is to say, for Religion, Papistrie or worse: for policie, a factious hart, a discoursing head, a mynde to medle in all mens matters: for experience, plentie of new mischieves never knowne in England before: for maners, varietie of vanities, and chaunge of filthy lyving. (78)

Ascham believed that Venetian courtesan bastards were so numerous that they could supply the Catholic Church! Yet Venice was a magnet for the relatively provincial English despite its perceived dangers. The city was sophisticated and stylish, and represented, perhaps more than any other single place, alluring worldly temptations of all sorts – licentiousness, salacious books and 'false' religion.

Thus, Venice is not only Shylock's Jewish world of getting and spending, but also by extension the Pope's Catholic 'Rome' as well. If Portia can be seen as the nubile 'queen' in fairyland Belmont, the Jew in turn is the 'Pope' in Venetian Rome. Shylock, that is, is symbolically more than a Jew: he is the composite 'bad angel,' alien-outsider, the 'other,' who represents the one in league with the devil, who is the tempter in Shakespeare's Anglican Protestant setting. The late sixteenth century was a time, we are told by James Shapiro and others, when England was trying to locate and define its national, racial and cultural identity, as well as continuing to insist on its uniquely religious one. One way to do this was to consider what the English were not. Jews, who had been banished in 1290 and were relatively few in number in early modern England (Shapiro estimates 'never more than a couple of hundred at any given time'),[21] obviously were not. Shapiro writes, 'Elizabethans considered Jews to be unlike themselves in terms of religion, race, nationality, and even sexuality' (3). Catholics, a constant challenge to Anglican and monarchical authority at home and from abroad, were also thought of by the orthodox at this time as not truly 'English.' Pope Pius V excommunicated the queen in 1570, dissolving her subjects' allegiance, and in turn Papism was deemed treasonable.[22]

English Protestants often accused Catholics of exhibiting Jewish tendencies. 'The Elizabethan word "Jew," ' according to Hunter, 'was a word of general abuse' (215). Shapiro notes in Martin Luther's commentary on Galatians (published in 1575) that the 'Papists are our Jews which molest us no less than the Jews did Paul' (quoted in Shapiro 21). There was ongoing and justifiable fear that Catholics from Portugal, Spain, Italy and Rome were infiltrating Protestant England, sometimes masquerading as Jews, in order to convert the queen's subjects and subvert the crown (Shapiro 27–28). Before the century's turn, England and, therefore, the Established Church could be easily perceived by its enemies as fragile and vulnerable. The queen was still unmarried, in her 60s, and long past child-bearing. It is no wonder then that late sixteenth-century English literature is replete with nervous anti-Catholic propaganda and satire.

Marlowe devotes two scenes in Act 3 of *Doctor Faustus* to satirizing the Pope and the ceremonies of Catholicism. Doctor Faustus 'long[s] to see the monuments / And situation of bright-splendent Rome' (3.1.50–51), and Mephistopheles obliges him with a tour of the city in recognizably tour-guide language:

> Know that this city stands upon seven hills
> That underprop the groundwork of the same:
> Just through the midst runs flowing Tiber's stream
> With winding banks that cut it in two parts,
> That make safe passage to each part of Rome.
> Upon the bridge called Ponte Angelo
> Erected is a castle passing strong
> Where thou shalt see such store of ordinance
> As that the double cannons forged of brass
> Do match the number of the days contained
> Within the compass of one complete year,
> Beside the gates and high pyramides
> That Julius Caesar brought from Africa. (3.1.33–46)

The two mischievously disrupt the Pope's 'solemnity,' and hear statements that the Pope 'cannot err' and 'all power on earth' is his (3.1.153, 152). The action dissolves into low comedy with the invisible Doctor Faustus speaking insults, snatching dishes and goblets, striking the Pope and friars, and climatically setting off firecrackers (3.2).

But Catholics and Jews were not the only perceived alien-devils. Any religious group outside the Established Church was suspect and at times labeled 'Judaizers,' to associate it with Judaism (Shapiro 21). In Elizabethan times, Protestant exiles who had come into contact with Calvinism, and other more local sects, developed the sober values associated with both Shylock and the Puritans. One John Traske was detained with his followers for Jewish leanings: he is described as 'first a puritan, then a separatist, and now is become a Jewish Christian' (quoted in Shapiro 23). The Scottish intellectual George Buchanan, tutor to the future King James I, was imprisoned by the Portuguese Inquisition 'on suspicion of Judaizing' (Shapiro

21). And Luther accused John Calvin himself of 'Judaizing' for denying the prophesy of the Virgin birth (Shapiro 22). Austere Protestant groups were particularly targeted. Some, in fact, invited their own trouble. Puritans, for example, considered themselves God's newly 'chosen people.' They self-consciously attempted to emulate Jewish ways and customs, giving themselves and their children Old Testament names, keeping kosher, observing a strict Sabbath and even undergoing circumcision in some cases. Such activities were eagerly noticed and exploited by Catholics and Anglicans alike. But, in turn, the Puritans 'looked upon the Anglican Church [as well as the Catholics] as idolatrous.'[23]

The established clergy and court advisors rightly understood that the Puritans posed a challenge and threat to the queen's authority. Their belief in and strict adherence to the Mosaic Code, for example, which included death for blasphemy or adultery, did not permit a merciful pardon by a temporal queen (STP 16–17). Indeed, 'Puritans as well as Jews were called devils in Shakespeare's time. ... The pious exterior of the Puritans, it was charged, concealed the spirit of the Devil.'[24] According to Wilhelm Creizenach, Jews and Puritans were afforded much the same treatment.[25]

Like Jews, Puritans were also usurers. Paul Siegel writes that 'Many of Shylock's traits would have reminded Shakespeare's audience of the Puritan usurers of its own time' (SPU 130). Shakespeare depended on them 'to associate Judaism, Puritanism, and usury' (STP 15). Playwright John Marston's *Satire II* (published 1598 but in circulation before) describes a Puritan moneylender who is worse than a Jew: 'No Jew, no Turk, would use a Christian / So inhumanely as this Puritan.'[26]

In his book *Shakespeare: The Invention of the Human*, Harold Bloom admits to being troubled most of all by Shylock's forced conversion in *The Merchant of Venice*. Yet like Portia, the Jew seems another character in the play who functions in part symbolically and thus is without choice. Bloom asks, 'Why did Shakespeare allow Antonio this final turn of the torturer's screw?'[27] Shylock's conversion, however, probably was perceived by Elizabethan audiences as a mercy, in that it offered the Jew the possibility of salvation. Additionally, the conversion might also have to do with when *Merchant* was written. Shakespeare composed his play just a few years before the turn of the seventeenth century. At this centennial time there was excited anticipation by Christians of all stripes, but especially Baptists, Quakers and other fundamentalist Protestant groups, of the imminent conversion of the Jews (Shapiro 28).

Shylock's agreeing to conversion, therefore, might have been seen as a symbolic fulfillment of the long-awaited and now imminent mass Jewish conversion. Too, Shylock is gone before the last act, a scene of poetry, music, harmony, playfulness, love in heavenly and Christian Belmont.

So then, the bad angel-devil Shylock can be seen as Pope and Puritan. Well, what about a Jewish Doctor Faustus? Shakespeare may have known the tradition of associating the Jewish Johan Fust, Johannes Gutenberg's financial backer and subsequent legal antagonist, with Doctor Faustus. Fust was thought to have stolen the Christian Bible printer's invention of moveable type. Additionally, Frances Yates calls attention to a Rembrandt etching, sometimes titled *The Inspired Scholar* (c. 1652, Figure 1), that is often interpreted to represent 'Faust and is depicting a profound search for forbidden knowledge.'[28] Indeed, the composition has come to be called *Faust in His Study, Watching a Magic Disc.* Although Yates discredits this identification, Kott views the pensive scholar as both Faust and Jew: 'Faust wears a wide, loose coat and has a nightcap or white turban on his head, much like those worn by the Jewish elders of Amsterdam in other paintings' (1). The bright 'magic disc' shining through the window contains the letters I N R I, the monogram of Christ, as well as a Hebrew anagram in the outer ring (Yates 187). Thus, the scholar's mystical vision might suggest an understanding of the limitations of his 'book,' and spiritual knowledge offered through conversion.

We have read *The Merchant of Venice* as a Faust play, demonstrating that *Doctor Faustus* has much in common with Shakespeare's comedy, a play composed when Marlowe's tragedy was popular on the stage. The Faust motif is clearly observable as an intertext in *Merchant,* placing characters with choices to make between two worlds, at times exhorted by good and bad angels, or identified with one or another of these worlds and its values. The hellish choice or identification involves over-concern with the here-and-now, suggested by the vengeful and profit-driven values of Shylock the Jew, who generalizes to all the 'alien-others' despised by the Elizabethan English. The Christian choice or identification, on the other hand, affirms the supposedly Anglican message, that the soul and eternity are more important than the body and this life, and that generosity, friendship, love, mercy and sacrifice are the correct values to have on this earth. Shakespeare, then, not only borrowed from Christopher Marlowe's *The Jew of Malta* for his Shylock play, but also, and significantly, from *Doctor Faustus* as well.

Figure 1. *Faust in His Study, Watching a Magic Disc*, Rembrandt. Photo Credit: Victoria and Albert Museum, London. By Permission of Art Resource, NY.

 Shakespeare's Prospero is, of course, the scholar who ultimately drowns his 'book' (*The Tempest*, 5.1.57). He is the 'white' magician teaching reconciliation and forgiveness, as opposed to Shylockian revenge and literalness or Doctor Faustus' self-serving 'black' magic. Roger Shattuck points out that 'The Latin Faustus means "the favored one," a form that can yield Prospero in English.' And he adds, 'It is instructive to read *The Tempest* as a modified Faust play.'[29] Indeed, *The Tempest* and not *The Merchant of Venice* is the Shakespeare play most often compared with Marlowe's *Doctor Faustus* (the *English Faust Book* editor notes four parallels with the Romance from Marlowe's source [Jones 258]). Both dramas contain banquet scenes, 'echo' scenes, play-within-plays and low comic actions that reflect events of high seriousness. Both have central magician characters with spirit servants (one good and one bad) aiding them.

One can also observe Shakespeare's use of a modified Faust pattern – a central character placed between two opposing appeals – in other plays as well, albeit more implicitly and subtly. In *Henry IV, Part 1*, for example, Hal is in a kind of Faust situation positioned between his 'bad angel' Falstaff and the courageous rebel Hotspur. Neither Sir John nor Harry Percy, of course, is purely good or bad. Though a coward, liar, thief and shameless exploiter, Falstaff is at the same time witty, engaging and a boon companion. Similarly, the honor-motivated Hotspur is impetuous, mercurial and disrespectful. However, morally complicated as they are, Falstaff and Hotspur represent a choice of models and values for Hal. He will ultimately reject Falstaff's perpetual 'holiday' fun and life-at-all-costs for responsibility and honor. In *Part 2* the prince eventually banishes the fat knight and the worldly excess and irresponsibility that he represents, in favor of assuming his birthright. He takes his designated place fulfilling his destiny. We know from almost the start of *Henry IV, Part 1* that Hal will choose properly. He will

> ... imitate the sun,
> Who doth permit the base contagious clouds
> To smother up his beauty from the world,
> That when he please again to be himself,
> Being wanted, he may be more wond'red at
> By breaking through the foul and ugly mists
> Of vapors that did seem to strangle him.
> ...
> [He'll] so offend, to make offence a skill,
> Redeeming time when men think least ... [he] will. (1.2.197–217)

Toward the end of the play, Shakespeare places Hal *physically* (and presumably visually) between his good and bad 'angels,' reminding reader or audience of his Faust-like situation. The prince then eulogizes both of his models. The vanquished Hotspur had a 'great heart [but he also had] / Ill-weav'd ambition' (5.4.87–88); his 'body did contain a spirit, / A kingdom for it was too small a bound'

(5.4.89–90). But then Hal notices Falstaff on the ground apparently
dead as well. He laments wittily, a tribute to his witty fat friend:

> What, old acquaintance! could not all this flesh
> Keep in a little life? Poor Jack, farewell!
> I could have better spar'd a better man.
> O, I should have a heavy miss of thee
> If I were much in love with vanity!
> …
> … in blood by noble Percy lie. (5.4.102–10)

Similarly, aspects of the Faust intertext can be seen, perhaps even
more clearly, in *Macbeth*. Both Macbeths have sold their souls to
the demonic forces of evil, represented by the witches. Like Faust
they pursue worldly ambition and power. Lady Macbeth's perverse
invocation to the 'spirits' to 'unsex' her and fill her 'from the crown
to the toe topful / Of direst cruelty' (1.5.38–54) anticipates her
husband's plea as he sets about to kill Banquo and Fleance: 'Come,
seeling night, / Scarf up the tender eye of pitiful day, / And with thy
bloody and invisible hand / Cancel and tear to pieces that great bond/
Which keeps me pale!' (3.2.46–50). Just as Shylock's 'house is hell,'
Macbeth's castle is also hell, as we learn from the Porter who imagines
himself at 'Hell Gate.' When Macduff and Lennox knock, the 'devil-
porter' responds, 'Who's there, / i' th' name of Belzebub?' (2.3.2,
3–4). Lady Macbeth and Macbeth's sterility – 'He has no children'
(4.3.216) – contrasting with Duncan's, Banquo's and Macduff's
offspring suggests the same sort of selfish focus on this world at the
expense of the next that can be found with Doctor Faustus, Shylock
and Falstaff. In the end, except for his significantly named servant
Seyton (read Satan), Macbeth, like Doctor Faustus, is alone. He has
given over his everlasting soul. His famous lines signal his despair:

> To-morrow, and to-morrow, and to-morrow,
> Creeps in this petty pace from day to day,
> To the last syllable of recorded time;
> And all our yesterdays have lighted fools
> The way to dusty death. Out, out brief candle!
> Life's but a walking shadow, a poor player,
> That struts and frets his hour upon the stage,
> And then is heard no more. It is a tale
> Told by an idiot, full of sound and fury,
> Signifying nothing. (5.5.19–28)

Other examples of variations on this Faust intertext might include *Antony and Cleopatra* and *Hamlet*. Mark Antony is placed between coldly Roman and warmly Egyptian values, Octavius Caesar and his sister Octavia and sexy Cleopatra, land and sea. Feeling both his age and overwhelming passion for Cleopatra, Antony compromises his warrior and responsible public self for personal pleasures of this world. He sacrifices Roman honor for indulgent and selfish love or perhaps lust. Similarly, Hamlet is caught between two value systems, one that asks him to avenge his father's murder and the other that teaches 'turn the other cheek.' Here we recall Shylock's revenge motive set against Christian teaching. To be sure, Hamlet has further choices to make, among them: 'To be, or not to be' (3.1.55). True, applying aspects of the Faust pattern to these plays is more of a stretch than what we have noticed in *The Merchant of Venice*, where it is explicit. However, Shakespeare seems to have internalized the Faust motif and returns to it with variations many times throughout his career.

Chapter 3
Two images: Coriolanus as Marsyas and Falstaff as Actaeon

Ovid, one of Shakespeare's favorite classical writers, tells the story of the satyr Marsyas' encounter with the god Apollo in the *Fasti* and *Metamorphoses*. Minerva (Pallas Athena in *Fasti*) fashions a flute. While playing it she observes her reflection in a stream, and seeing her 'girlish cheeks puffed out' concludes that such a distorted look is 'Too high a price for art.'[1] Disgusted, she casts off the instrument and curses anyone who might find it. Marsyas chances upon the flute and, remembering the goddess' music, it gives the satyr the reputation of a master musician, the equal of Apollo. Swelled with pride, Marsyas challenges the god to a musical duel, the winner of the contest choosing a punishment for the loser. Apollo is victorious and elects to flay Marsyas alive.

Myths were read allegorically in early modern England.[2] Arthur Golding's dedication to his translation of Ovid's *Metamorphoses* (1567), for example, which Shakespeare knew and used again and again, speaks of stories that contain 'pitthye, apt and pleyne / Instructions which import the prayse of vertues, and the shame / Of vices, with the due reqardes of eyther of the same.'[3] Thus, in his dedicatory 'Epistle' Golding interprets the story of the flaying of Marsyas to mean: 'no wyght should strive with God in word or thought / Nor deede. But [, he adds,] pryde and fond desyre of prayse have ever wrought / Confusion too the parties which accompt of them doo make' (Rouse 3). An individual may be stripped more than naked when challenging a god; he or she may be exposed in a most horrible way. In Ovid's words by way of Golding, Marsyas' punishment was

> one whole wounde. The griesly bloud did spin
> From every part, the sinewes lay discovered to the eye,
> The quivering veynes without a skin lay beating nakedly.
> The panting bowels in his bulke ye might have numbred well,
> And in his brest the shere small strings a man might easly tell.
>   (Rouse 128)

The challenger is tortured. In this case, his insides are turned outside because of the pride inherent in imitating a god's powers. George Sandys, Ovid's seventeenth-century translator and commentator, observes sagely that 'The fiction of the Satyres punishment was invented ... to deterre from such selfe-exaltation.'[4] Marsyas, he instructs, is an example of 'ambition and vaine-glory' (296).

Ovid's Minerva, the flute inventor, was also the 'warlike goddess [who] delights in drawn swords' (Nagle 102). In ancient Rome during the Spring equinox (March 19–22), she was honored together with the war god Mars in the five-day *Quinquatrus* festival. Shakespeare's Caius Martius is a soldier and not a musician, but he certainly is god-challenging proud. So described in the first scene of *Coriolanus* (1.1.39), his pride is reiterated throughout the play. The tribune Sicinius Velutus asks, 'Was ever man so proud as is this Martius?' (1.1.252), and his colleague Junius Brutus replies, 'Being mov'd, he will not spare to gird the gods' (1.1.256). Brutus later remarks to Coriolanus, 'You speak a'th'people / As if you were a god to punish, not / A man of their infirmity' (3.1.80–82). Even Coriolanus' spiritual father Menenius Agrippa concurs: 'His nature is too noble for the world; / He would not flatter Neptune for his trident, / Or Jove for's power to thunder' (3.1.254–56). Perhaps most telling is Menenius' further characterization: 'He wants nothing of a god but eternity and a heaven to throne in' (5.4.23–24). Coriolanus himself declares that he will 'stand / As if a man were author of himself, / And knew no other kin' (5.3.35–37), a sure sentiment for a tragic consequence. Like the proud satyr Marsyas, the proud warrior Martius is a god challenger.

The names of the soldier and satyr are, to be sure, near homophones in English. Marsyas possibly comes from the Greek *marnamai* for 'battler,'[5] and Mars, the god of war, is obviously invoked in the given name of Coriolanus. This latter association is made clear when a Volscian servingman speaks of Coriolanus' welcome by his former enemy as if 'he were son and heir to Mars' (4.5.191–92). Caius Martius appeals by name to the war god when he is ready to attack Corioli early in the play (1.4.10), and Tullus Aufidius taunts Coriolanus late in the tragedy when Martius again appeals to Mars (5.6.99). Jonathan Bate observes that 'Shakespeare's audience would ... have been adept in the art of recognizing classical allusions, whether they were highly self-conscious, as in some of the early works, or woven more subtly into the text, as in the later plays' (20). Martius and Marsyas seem more than coincidentally linked when one notices, as Bate does in a footnote (202, n.48), the reference to

Caius Martius as 'flea'd' (i.e. 'flayed') when he is described emerging from Corioli: 'Who's yonder, / That does appear as he were "*flea'd*"? O gods, / *He has the stamp of Martius*' (1.6.21–23, emphasis mine). Shakespeare's Plutarch source does not tell of Caius Martius entering the city by himself and emerging as if 'flea'd.'

If Shakespeare was indeed thinking of Marsyas' punishment when he describes Martius in this scene, might he have been prompted by Titian's painting *The Flaying of Marsyas* (Figure 2), the artist's late work dating from the 1570s, in addition to the *Metamorphoses*? Ovid was an important sourcebook for the painter as well as the playwright, and Titian painted a number of so-called *poesie* for his patron Philip II of Spain, including a *Venus and Adonis* and *Tarquin and Lucretia*, among other Ovidian subjects (for example, *Perseus and Andromeda*, *Diana and Actaeon* and *Diana and Callistro*). Shakespeare and Titian thus had a number of mythic source stories in common. Additionally, as Sydney Freedberg notes, 'The late Titian's visual language works upon us as supreme literary language does – as in Shakespeare, for obvious example,'[6] and Jaromir Neumann sees in Titian's *The Flaying of Marsyas* 'A tragic vision of human conflict, worthy of the genius of Shakespeare.'[7]

Titian may have chosen his flaying subject because of a contemporary historical event, an event I have noted as likely in the background of *Much Ado About Nothing* and *Othello*.[8] The Turkish siege of Famagusta on Cyprus, from September 18, 1570 to August 1571, resulted in an ignominious end for Marc Antonio Bragadino, Captain of this Venetian outpost (see Freedberg 62–63). Bragadino's nose and ears were cut off, he was paraded before the Turkish troops on hands and knees, forced to bear dirt and stones, and, ultimately, he was flayed alive before the Turkish general. The cruelty of this event was the talk of Christian Europe and in some measure prompted the Battle of Lepanto on October 7, 1571, an event recorded by Titian in his *Allegory of the Battle of Lepanto* painting for Philip II of Spain. Pope Pius V managed to get Venice and Spain to cooperate and form a 'Holy League' alliance to wage war against 'the heathens of the East,' a sort of final Crusade that even Protestant England applauded.

It is possible that Shakespeare saw Titian's *The Flaying of Marsyas* or a sketch of it (Cornelius Cort and Niccolo Boldrini engraved many of Titian's images, though this particular one is not recorded). The painting was a part of the famous Arundel collection of Thomas Howard, second Earl of Arundel, listed in an inventory of 1655 after the death of his wife Aletheia (the inventory also included another

Figure 2. *The Flaying of Marsyas*, Titian. Archbishop's Palace, Kromeriz, Czech Republic. Photo Credit: Erich Lessing. By Permission of Art Resources, NY.

Apollo and Marsyas painting by an unidentified artist). Arundel's wife was the daughter of Gilbert Talbot, seventh Earl of Shrewsbury, who had traveled to Italy in 1570, around the time Titian was likely working on *The Flaying of Marsyas*.[9] Arundel himself, encouraged by Shrewsbury's and his own love of Italian art, possibly visited Italy in 1609,[10] and he definitely travelled there in 1612. On this last visit, David Howarth writes, 'Nothing is known of what purchases were made by Arundel in Venice, but it can be assumed that he was ... acquisitive' (37). There is also the possibility that the Titian painting may have come into the Arundel collection earlier, either by way of Shrewsbury (perhaps as a part of Aletheia's dowry in 1605) or as an inheritance from John, Lord Lumley, 'a great collector' (Howarth 10). Lumley had married into the Arundel line and died in 1609, and his collection passed to Thomas in 1617 (Howarth 10). However, there is no mention of the painting in the Lumley inventory.[11] Most scholars conjecture, without definitive documentary evidence, that *The Flaying of Marsyas* was purchased during the Howards' 1620 visit to Italy or even later.[12] Neumann writes,

> We know that the Countess of Arundel lived in a village not far from Venice after the year 1620 and had personal contact with Titianello, the artist's nephew, who in 1622 dedicated to her the biography of Titian written by an unknown author. Many facts seem to indicate that *The Flaying of Marsyas* was purchased from a Venetian or other Italian collection to which it might have come straight from the artist's collection at his death. (9–10)

Thomas Howard's ancestors included Thomas Mowbray, Duke of Norfolk, who Shakespeare portrays in his *Richard II*, and the poet Henry Howard, Earl of Surrey, famous for his sonnets. The Howard family had been theater company patrons for a number of generations,[13] and Thomas' father Philip (1557–95) was patron to a company that acted at the Curtain Theater in the 1580s.[14] Philip Howard, once a favorite of Queen Elizabeth, came to be on the wrong side during the religious conflicts of his time and died in the Tower. Philip was canonized a Roman Catholic saint in 1970.[15] Philip's art-collector son Thomas, born when the father was in prison and whom he never saw because he would not renounce Catholicism and take the Anglican Communion, succeeded to the Arundel title in 1604 (Howarth 5–7). There is record of a 1610 appearance of Thomas' theater company at Leicester (Murray 1: 20–21). Both Arundel and his lady were frequent participants in the masques at the court of King James and Queen Anne, where they had contact both with Ben Jonson and Inigo Jones, among other theater people (Hervey 36, 53). The Countess Arundel, for example, is listed among the 'celebrators' for Jonson and Jones' *Masque of Queens* in February 1609 at Whitehall.[16] King James was godfather to the Arundels' first-born son, who was named in the king's honor (Hervey 36).

The precise dating of *Coriolanus* is problematic, with only stylistic evidence and a few dubious contemporary references to go on. Philip Brockbank, the New Arden editor, places the play between 1605 and 1610, but agrees with E.K. Chambers that a date toward

the end of the decade is likely.[17] Since Arundel was a patron of
players and himself acted in court masques, he conceivably could
have come into contact with Shakespeare either before or when he
was writing *Coriolanus*. Another connection linking the Earl and
the playwright is that Shakespeare's patron Henry Wriothesley, third
Earl of Southampton, was related to the Howard family through
his mother (Hervey 42). In addition, the playwright's company
at this time was the 'King's Men,' and Arundel was an intimate
of King James. So there is the possibility that Shakespeare knew
Arundel, and the further possibly that he saw *The Flaying of Marsyas*
or a sketch of it when writing *Coriolanus*. In any case, the painter's
work sounds themes similar to ones in several of Shakespeare's late
plays: for example, the consequences of overreaching pride, as in
Coriolanus, and the artist's possible reflective farewell to his art, as in
The Tempest.

Titian's painting is worth looking at closely. The nearly life-size
figures around the central image in *The Flaying of Marsyas* have been
variously interpreted by art historians. Presumably Apollo is the one
doing the skinning, aided by satyrs who perhaps represent jealous
and unappreciative fellow creatures always ready to turn on the artist
(compare the Roman citizens' and tribunes' attitude toward their
warrior hero in *Coriolanus*). The figure to the left, looking up and
playing the Renaissance *lira da braccio*, is thought by Philipp Fehl
to represent either Marsyas' pupil Olympus, who claimed Marsyas'
body for burial;[18] or a servant to Apollo, who holds his lyre while
the god does the flaying; or even a second image of Apollo himself.
This Apollo could be singing the flaying story; the painting, in
Fehl's words, might be 'a picture within a picture' (1410). Neumann
agrees that the *lira* player is Apollo; however, he interprets the figure
as follows: 'the victorious Apollo gazing in musical ecstasy towards
the heavens is not merely a reference to the preceding contest with
Marsyas; it is also (even mainly) a depiction of that state of divine
harmony in which the soul is freed from terrestrial bonds' (22–23).
Using x-radiography A. Gentili found that an Apollo holding a
lyre had been painted out where this other figure is now placed
(Rosenberg 370). Interestingly, the current musician's face bears
a striking resemblance to the face of Titian's *St. Sebastian*, a work
of the artist's same late period. While Gentili finds this association
enigmatic (Rosenberg 370), Marsyas' mythic martyrdom might be
seen as a parallel to Saint Sebastian's Christian martyrdom: both saint
and satyr challenged Roman gods and were destroyed (Rosenberg
370).[19] As Harold E. Wethey notes, 'The gory execution [of Marsyas

in *The Flaying*] is presented in the same spirit as the martyrdom of a Christian saint.'[20]

The *lira da braccio* player substitution for the earlier Apollo with lyre image might also suggest that Titian wished the new scene to represent an allegory of the artist at various stages of a career or even Titian's own artistic career. The cherub to the right would then suggest the child that will develop into the artist, the *lira* musician looking toward the heavens is the mature artist practicing his art, and the old man with eyes downcast represents the artist at the end of his life. This old man is thought to be a self-portrait, reminiscent of the 1567–68 painting in the Prado (Rosenberg 370). The figure is also identified as King Midas (note the crown), who had insisted that Pan was a better musician than Apollo in another musical contest (often conflated with the Marsyas duel) and thus earned asses ears, though these are not to be seen in Titian's painting (see *Meta.* Book XI; Fehl 1405). The dejected expression on the face of the Midas self-portrait might reflect Titian's questioning the value of a mortal's dedicated life of art in terms of the punishment it exacts, represented by the flaying image at the center of the composition. However, Neumann believes that 'Midas – Titian – is meditating on the victory of divine art, for it was to that art that he devoted all his interest' (24). Wethey suggests more generally that 'The highly sympathetic mood in the presentation of Midas gives the impression that Titian himself shared Midas' reflection on the cruelty with which fate so often afflicts mankind' (93). In any case, the allegory of the proud artist's life and its continual hardships and demands in the service of the unappreciative masses, then ultimate sacrifice, might be in part compared to the tragic life-story of the proud warrior of Shakespeare's *Coriolanus.* The theme that pride will have its fall is common to both the painting and the play.

The only artist that Shakespeare mentions by name in the plays is Giulio Romano, 'that rare Italian master,' in *The Winter's Tale*: 'had he himself eternity and could put breath into his work, [he] would beguile Nature her custom, so perfectly he is her ape' (5.2.97–100). Simon Forman saw *The Winter's Tale* at the Globe on May 15, 1611, and the New Arden editor J.H.P. Pafford hypothesizes that it was written in the early months of that year; that is, probably shortly after *Coriolanus*.[21] Giulio is the named sculptor of the Hermione 'statue,' the figure that comes to life in the manner of the statue in Ovid's Pygmalion story (see *Meta.* Book X). But Frederick Hartt points out, 'we do not have a single record of a work of sculpture from Giulio Romano's hands,'[22] so it seems that Shakespeare has

metamorphosized Giulio in his play from architect and painter to
sculptor. Yet the Arden editor observes that Giulio's tomb inscription
indicates that he was also a sculptor (Pafford 150, n.96). Further,
'The epitaph goes on to say that Jupiter carried Julio off because
he could not tolerate being surpassed in artistic work by a mortal'
(Pafford 150, n.96) – again the proud artist and the angry god
theme.

Giulio's masterpiece, the Plazzo del Te in Mantua, which he
designed, built and decorated for Federico II Gonzaga, contains a
room, the Sala di Ovidio, devoted to frescos depicting scenes from
Ovid's *Metamorphoses*. Among them is the damaged *The Flaying of
Marsyas*, reputed to be Titian's inspiration for his own rendering of
the myth (Wethey 3: 92). A preliminary pen and bistre wash sketch
for this fresco is now in the Louvre (Figure 3). The sketch and
Titian's painting differ in some relatively minor details: in Titian
Marsyas' body is turned more toward the viewer, two dogs and a
child are added, one satyr wears a hat, the background is filled in
(see Fehl 1405). However, the compositions are very similar overall,
especially in the figures depicted and their dispositions. Both have
Marsyas strung to a tree upside down, a detail unlike previous
pictorial rendering of the myth, for example the one by Giulio's
teacher Raphael (Hartt 111). Another room in the Gonzaga villa,
the Sala di Atilio Regulus, has a ceiling illustration that may picture
Gaius Marcius Coriolanus Discovered Among the Volscians (Figure 4).[23]
If this apparently nineteenth-century identification of Coriolanus is
correct, bringing Marsyas and Coriolanus together in one structure
would be an interesting coincidence in that it was effected by the
only artist specifically named by Shakespeare, and involves reference
to two of his plays likely written within a year or two of each
other.

It is tempting to speculate that Shakespeare traveled to Mantua
– the birthplace of Castiglione, and a city mentioned in *The Two
Gentlemen of Verona*, *The Taming of the Shrew* and *Romeo and Juliet*
– and visited Giulio Romano's magnificent Plazzo del Te. Or that
he visited Venice and saw Titian's painting. But the consensus is
that he did not (see Levith 87–90). However, he may have heard
reports about the Gonzaga villa (perhaps from Arundel, Inigo Jones
or other travelers) or have seen sketches of the Marsyas fresco and/or
possible Martius ceiling, just as he may have had contact with the
Titian image. What is not conjectural is that Shakespeare knew Ovid
both in Latin and in Golding's translation of the *Metamorphoses*
and found the Marsyas story there. Moreover, the coincidence of

Figure 3. *The Flaying of Marsyas*, Giulio Romano. Louvre, Paris, France. Photo Credit: Réunion des Musées Nationaux. By Permission of Art Resource, NY.

Figure 4. Giulio Romano (Giulio Pippi), *Gaius Marcius Coriolanus Discovered Among the Volscians*, Yale University Art Gallery, Maitland F. Griggs, B.A., 1896 and Everett V. Meeks, B.A. 1901 Funds.

the names Martius and Marsyas and the flayed image of the proud
warrior who challenges the gods and gets punished for his *hubris*
suggests that Shakespeare was deliberately allusive. Bate affirms that
'Shakespeare was an extremely intelligent and sympathetic reader of
Ovid and … his readings are imbedded in his own works' (13).

In a happy phrase, Francis Meres writes in his *Palladis Tamia: Wit's
Treasury,* 'As the soule of *Euphorbus* was thought to live in *Pythagoras,*
so the sweete wittie soule of *Ovid* lives in mellifluous & hony-
tongued *Shakespeare.*'[24] Meres' is speaking here specifically about
the poet's *Venus and Adonis, The Rape of Lucrece* and Shakespeare's
'sug'red sonnets.' However, Meres goes on to praise the playwright's
comedies and tragedies, likening them to the achievement of the
Latin Plautus and Seneca. Writing in 1598, Meres does not include
the yet-to-be written *Coriolanus,* which, in the words of the New
Arden editor Philip Brockbank, 'is remarkable for its apparently
close dependence upon one soverign source: "The Life of Caius
Martius Coriolanus", in *The Lives of the Noble Grecians and Romans,*
translated "out of Greeke into French by James Amyot" and "out of
French into Englishe by Thomas North"' (29). But the 'Tale of the
Belly' and other play moments suggest Shakespeare's wide reading
and recall what was brought to bear on his late tragedy.

*   *   *   *

A further example of a stage image and various possible intertexts
is Sir John Falstaff as Actaeon in *The Merry Wives of Windsor.* This
association was noted by Geoffrey Bullough and further elaborated
by John M. Steadman, who argues that in the final act 'The analogy
[of Herne the Hunter] with the Actaeon myth is inescapeable.'[25]
Jeanne Addison Roberts, on the other hand, is skeptical, and calls
the identification 'puzzling.'[26] Toward the end of Shakespeare's
English comedy, the wives convince Falstaff to meet them costumed
as Herne the Hunter by the oak in the woods outside Windsor.
Mistress Page relates what seemingly is a local legend:

> There is an old tale goes, that Herne the Hunter
> (Sometime a keeper here in Windsor forest)
> Doth all the winter-time, at still midnight,
> Walk round about an oak, with great ragg'd horns,
> And there he blasts the tree, and takes the cattle,
> And [makes] milch-kinde yield blood, and shakes a chain
> In a most hideous and dreadful manner.
> You have heard of such a spirit, and well you know

> The superstitious idle-headed eld
> Receiv'd and did deliver to our age
> This tale of Herne the Hunter for a truth. (4.4.28–38)[27]

Bullough notes the uncertainty of this folk tale, and speculates that probably Shakespeare invented it (17). He also remarks the significance of the 1602 Quarto's naming of the spirit '*Horne* [rather than 'Herne,' but perhaps heard as a homophone from the stage] the Hunter,' which reinforces the cuckoldry theme with Sir John, not Ford or Page, victimized. Falstaff's 'buck' (laundry) basket, as well, anticipates his later 'buck' (stag) horns.

T.W. Craik, the 1989 Oxford editor, calls attention to the fact that the Quarto and Folio versions of the play differ significantly, and that the Quarto should be regarded only 'as a guide.'[28] The Quarto is confusing, for example, as to what may be intended for Sir John's Herne disguise. Mistress Page declares at one point, '*Horne* the hunter ... walkes in Shape of a great Stagge,'[29] but Sir Hugh Evans states Falstaff's 'bodie [is] man, his head a buck' (Melchiori 320). Indeed, several stage directions in the Quarto also suggest that Falstaff should be wearing a stag mask: '*Enter sir Iohn with a Bucks head vpon him*' (Melchiori 319); '*Falstaffe pulles of his bucks head, and rises up*' (Melchiori 320). The question, then, is this: is Falstaff intended to be sporting a full head mask or merely antlers for his disguise? Craik notes that the *OED* explains a 'buck's head' as a technical term for a buck's antlers (227), which Mistress Page refers to as 'these fair yokes' (5.5.107) in the Folio version. On Sir John's head, they serve as proof that Falstaff is 'a cuckoldly knave' (5.5.110); rather than planting cuckolds' horns on Ford and Page, as Sir John would, he places them on his own head, symbolic of his lustful animal nature and ultimate defeat at the hands of the merry wives.

Bullough lists as a 'probable source' the Actaeon story specifically from Ovid's *Metamorphoses*:[30] 'Actaeon had become a cant name for a cuckold, as [one of] two references in the play show' (17). Ford calls Page 'a secure and willful Actaeon' (3.2.43), and Pistol describes Falstaff 'With liver burning hot ... Like Sir Actaeon he, with Ringwood [his dog] at thy heels' (2.1.117–18), associating Actaeon with lust. Again in *Titus Andronicus*, when Bassianus and Lavinia discover the lustful queen Tamora and her lover Aaron the Moor in the forest, an Actaeon reference is invoked to suggest their lust (2.3.63). Though John M. Steadman agrees that the Actaeon myth may, indeed, be the inspiration for Herne the Hunter (231), and elaborates the identification, he argues reasonably that 'the question of specific influence is … complex' (237). Steadman hypothesizes that Falstaff probably is not meant by Shakespeare to be costumed as a complete animal as in Ovid. Diana

> … by and by doth spread
> a payre of lively olde Harts hornes upon his [Actaeon's] sprinckled head.
> She sharpes his eares, she makes his necke both slender, long and lanke.
> She turnes his fingers into feete, his armes to spindle shanke
> She wrappes him in a hairie hyde beset with speckled spottes,
> And planteth in him fearfulnesse. And so away he trottes. (*Meta.* 3. 229–34)

Rather, Falstaff's disguise seems to Steadman closer to the more general Renaissance iconography of the myth; that is to say, a human body with stag horns (231). Steadman relates the myth to the Renaissance interpretation that Actaeon's 'horns are an emblematic expression of lust and its chastisement' (234). He notes Golding's warning in his prefactory epistle to his dedicatee, the Earl of Leicester, that Actaeon's fate will come to those who pursue 'foule excesse of chamberworke' (quoted in Steadman 236). The critic also sees Falstaff's other transformations as 'conventional symbols of "unchaste desire"' (237).

However, what is even more problematic with the Falstaff/ Actaeon identification are the questions raised by Roberts:

> Why should Falstaff, the fat dissolute old knight, be associated with the young hunter, the nephew of Cadmus, who comes by accident upon Diana bathing, is changed into a stag and torn to pieces by his own dogs? Why should Actaeon be associated with adultery, and in what sense can he be seen as representing a moral lesson? It may be true that Actaeon came to be associated with adultery because of his horns, but neither he nor Falstaff fits the prototype of the horned husband. (75–76)

Roberts justly concludes that in the story 'Actaeon simply happened to be in the wrong place at the wrong time' (76); that is, unlike Actaeon with Diana, Sir John does not chance upon the wives but seeks them out, and he is not a victim as in Ovid of 'cruell fortune' or 'cruell fate' (3.165, 208). Falstaff is motivated by a lack of income and his object is the wives' family money which he deliberately pursues from the start. Seduction of the wives is what he thinks will achieve his goal. In addition, Sir John is neither eaten by dogs nor, for that matter, comes to any other bad end. Rather, Page kindly invites him to dinner at the close of the comedy.

The 'purification' of Falstaff is understood to have taken place by then. Sir John represents a decayed, dishonorable and careless knighthood within the new middle-class society. At the very start of the play, the enraged Justice Shallow establishes Falstaff's cavalier and irresponsible attitude. Justice Shallow, a Gloucester 'gentleman' who fought with a 'long sword' in former days, and is just one rank himself below knight (Melchiori 124 n.3), first accuses Sir John of unacceptable behavior: 'Knight, you have beaten my men, kill'd my deer, and broke open my lodge' (1.1.111–12). Sir John's casual retort and admission – 'But not kiss'd your keeper's daughter? … I have done all this' (1.1.113, 115) – shows him unrepentant. Moreover, Falstaff's followers have abused Shallow's relative. Slender complains, 'They carried me to the tavern and made me drunk, and afterward pick'd my pocket' (1.1.125–27). Falstaff is desperate for funds to sustain his now antiquated lifestyle, and will stoop to anything to satisfy his needs. Sir John's situation has come about because the feudal economic sub-structure that supported him (as the supposed 'honorable' king's soldier) and his servants has passed, and with it, as shown during the previous time-period reflected in the *Henry IV* plays, Sir John's aristocratic honor and morality. Falstaff has no visible means of support for himself, and, as we see, cannot now afford his fellows: 'Truly, mine host, I must turn away some of my followers' (1.3.4–5). He must fend for himself now: 'There is no remedy; I must cony-catch, I must shift' (1.3.33–34). His plan, therefore, is to get at Ford and Page's wealth by seducing their wives. His vanity and knighthood make him confident about his charm-appeal for what he perceives as these susceptible and 'lower-class' women. After all, he is a gallant with refined manners and education. In a play mostly in middle-class prose, dialect and accent, he can speak wittily and write more-or-less gracefully. He promises Mistress Ford, that he 'would make … [her his] lady' (3.3.51), and kisses her in greeting: 'by my troth, you are very well met. By your leave, good mistress' (1.1.192–93).

The merry wives, of course, take it upon themselves to comically purge Sir John of his libertine and decadent aristocratic morality and confirm their bourgeois values, which include faithfulness ('honesty') in marriage and exposing Falstaff's would-be attempts at seduction which would compromise Windsor's social order. Will-he or nil-he, they would comically purify this dishonorable and sinful knight, so that he and his kind might be more acceptable to fold into the new middle-class moral order. To do this the wives parody the rituals of baptism by water, exorcism by beating and chasing away bodily demons by torment and fire.[31] Shakespeare here might be satirizing specifically Catholic rituals, as there was around this time a national campaign against so-called Papist superstition. (A few years after Shakespeare's play, Samuel Harsnett's book *A Declaration of Egregious Popish Impostors* [1603] specifically attacked exorcism as practiced by the Jesuits.)

First, Falstaff is put in a buck basket amidst the 'dirty linen,' to be thrown out with the laundry. Mistress Ford's instructions to her servants are to 'carry it among the whitsters [clothes bleachers] in Datchet-mead, and there empty it in the muddy ditch close by the Thames side' (3.3.14–16). She continues to Mistress Page, 'I am half afraid he will have a need of washing, so throwing him into the water will do him a benefit' (3.3.182–84). Sir John later laments, 'to be thrown in the Thames. ... I have a kind of alacrity in sinking; [and] the bottom were as deep as hell, I should drown' (3.5.5–6, 12–14). However, this first 'baptism' seemingly has no effect on Sir John's behavior, and spurred on by Ford disguised as Brooke, Falstaff is, once again, encouraged to attempt to seduce Mistress Ford. His sinful demons still possess him. To escape Ford's house a second time, the wives dress Falstaff as Mother Prat (whose name suggests 'buttocks' *OED*), the witch of Brainford (Brentford in some editions) (4.2.98). Prompted by Mistress Ford – 'Nay, good, sweet husband! Good gentlemen, let him [not] strike the old woman' (4.2.180–81) – her husband cudgels Sir John soundly, and Falstaff later tells Brooke, 'he beat me grievously, in the shape of a woman' (5.1.20–21). 'I was beaten myself into all colors of the rainbow; and I was like to be apprehended for the witch of Brainford' (4.5.115–17). Following this comic exorcism, Mistress Ford declares, 'I'll have the cudgel hallow'd and hung o'er the altar; it hath done meritorious service' (4.2.204–05).

Falstaff's final punishment to rid him of his sinful demons is his pinching and burning as Herne the Hunter in Windsor woods. Mistress Page instructs: 'Let the supposed fairies pinch him sound, / And burn him with their tapers' (4.4.62–63), and Mistress Quickly, as Queen of Fairies, orders, 'With trial-fire touch me his finger-end. / If he be chaste, the flame will back descend / And turn him to no pain; but if he start, / It is the flesh of a corrupted heart' (5.5.84–87).

Falstaff finally comes to understand that his actions are unacceptable in Windsor society and seems chastened by his several ordeals: 'I do begin to perceive that I am made an ass' (5.5.119), Ford adding, 'Ay, and an ox too' (5.5.120). He has been both vain and behaving in an uncivilized and animalistic manner. Sir John in the end seems to take the lessons to heart and acknowledges: 'Well, I am your theme' (5.5.161). He has learned and will reform. In turn, Page invites him to what might be thought of as a 'communion' dinner: 'Yet be cheerful, knight. Thou shalt eat a posset to-night at my house' (5.5.170–71). *The Merry Wives of Windsor* is, as Craik would have it, 'a comedy of forgiveness and reconciliation' (25). At the end, Falstaff is included in the company, not excluded from it like so many of Shakespeare's 'left over' characters from the comedies (Malvolio, Don John, Jacques, Antonio, etc.). And, while the image of Falstaff with horns may indeed recall Actaeon and his story in a fairly loose way for some members of Shakespeare's audience, Falstaff experiences a very different and ultimately inclusive happy fate.

But what of Fenton, the other aristocratic character in the play? Where does he fit in, and why does he get Anne Page – the girl everyone wants? Fenton, it turns out, plays a key role in the order of Windsor's middle-class society. Like Falstaff, in the past he has been a buddy of the wild Prince Hal and Poins. Page objects to his aristocratic birth, which implies libertine behavior, as well as Fenton's 'state being gall'd with … expense,' he 'seek[s] to heal it only by … [Page's] wealth' (3.4.5–6). Fenton, like Falstaff, needs financial support. He admits to Anne that he is first attracted to her because of her family money: 'I will confess thy father's wealth / Was the first motive that I woo'd thee, Anne' (3.4.13–14). However, he has subsequently fallen in love with her: 'Yet, wooing thee, I found thee of more value / Than stamps in gold, or sums in sealed bags; / And 'tis the very riches of thyself/ That now I aim at' (3.4.15–18). Their marriage at the end of *The Merry Wives of Windsor* signals Anne as one of the new merry wives; she is a clever woman who marries above her station and presumably for love. She will not have the foreign Dr. Caius, 'by Gar,' preferred by her mother, or the wealthy fool Slender – 'a world of vild ill-favor'd faults / Looks handsome in three hundred pounds a year!' (3.4.32–33) – favored by her father. Anne and Fenton's offspring will combine the graciousness and honor associated with the old aristocracy together with the good humor, practicality and bourgeois morality of the new social order.

Chapter 4
A Midsummer Night's Dream
and the Theseus myth

T.W. Craik writes that '*The Merry Wives of Windsor* and *A Midsummer Night's Dream* are as different from each other as any two of [Shakespeare's] ... comedies, but there can be no doubt that his earlier fairy play was in his mind when he was planning the end of this [later] one.'[1] In addition, both comedies lack a single textual source that combines the various elements of Shakespeare's multi-faceted plots. *The Merry Wives of Windsor* has no one pre-text that brings together Falstaff's antics with the merry wives, the wooing of Anne Page and her various suitors, the Latin lesson and foreign and domestic dialect humor and so on. Similarly, no single source text has been found for *A Midsummer Night's Dream* that contains Theseus and Hippolyta's wedding, young lovers courting and cavorting in the woods, Bottom's antics and the *Pyramus and Thisbe* play, and Oberon and Titania's woodland fairy world. While John Lyly may have cued Falstaff's burning and pinching in *The Merry Wives* and provided *Dream* with the prompt for 'balancing a number of self-contained groups, one against the other,'[2] Shakespeare himself seems to have been responsible for the imaginative juxtaposition of his specific groupings in both comedies. Furthermore, the playwright's suggested sources and analogues for *Dream* – according to Geoffrey Bullough, Arden editor Harold Brooks and others – are incredibly varied, ranging from Ovid to Plutarch to Chaucer to Berners to Scot to Adlington to Spenser to school and folk materials and even to Shakespeare himself.[3] Stephen Lynch puts it this way: 'the sources for *Midsummer Night's Dream* ... are so diverse that it is extremely difficult to discern at any point what Shakespeare is adapting and transforming. [The comedy] seems ... based indirectly on a variety of sources, none of them very close to the play.'[4]

On the other hand, Barbara A. Mowat argues that Shakespeare adapted specific Theseus story details from mostly three prompts to construct his own coherent version of the confusing quasi-historical character to be found in *Dream*: Theseus' character is 'woven

38

together from words, details, "facts," whose local habitations were in large part others' texts ... to give us *this* Theseus [of *Dream*], the Theseus who has won Hippolyta with his sword, who rises up early to do his observation to May, whose hounds are bred out of the Spartan kind, who scoffs at antique fables.'⁵ Mowat continues:

> The name 'Theseus' ... seems to have lived in print in Renaissance England chiefly in three texts: in Thomas North's translation (of Amyot's translation) of Plutarch's 'Life of Theseus' (the first of the *Lives of the Noble Grecians and Romanes*, published in England in 1579); in Chaucer's Knight's Tale (the first of the *Canterbury Tales*, published in England in 1532 as edited by Thynne); and in several passages in Ovid's *Metamorphoses* (published often in Latin and, as translated by Arthur Golding, published first in 1567). Each of these texts reflects a long history of documentation and commentary on 'Theseus.' (336)

Mowat acknowledges that other 'cues' may contribute to *Dream*'s Theseus' characterization (Reginald Scot's scorn of 'antique fables,' for instance), but she foregrounds as most important the ones she highlights. And despite what seems to others to be *Dream*'s ever-expanding range of discovered intertexts, one clearly encounters a dominant Theseus narrative. In Shakespeare's reflexive comedy concerning courtship, love and marriage, *A Midsummer Night's Dream* plays centrally and cleverly with details of the Theseus myth.⁶ Though Theseus appears in only three scenes and speaks only 233 lines in the play (1.1; 4.1; 5.1), his story holds the comedy together.

The 'local habitation,' a number of character names and various plot details in *Dream* point to the myth as one certain intertext. Just as in the myth, Shakespeare sets his play in Athens and its woodland environs where Theseus rules as duke. The names Hippolyta, Egeus, Bottom and Helena also recall the Greek hero's legend. Shakespeare's frame story concerns Theseus' court wedding to the Amazon Hippolyta (confused with Antiopa in some versions of the story),⁷ whom the duke, we are told, has won with his sword. In the myth, this sword (designed to test his strength), together with sandals or 'a pair of shoes' (North 13), the young Theseus discovers under a rock, and it identifies him as Egeus' heir and future ruler of Athens.

Chaucer writes in 'The Knight's Tale,' 'No man myghte gladden Theseus, / Savynge his olde fader Egeus.'⁸ But while Egeus [Aegeus] is Theseus' father in the myth, he is, of course, Hermia's in the play.⁹ The unfortunate mythic Egeus is blamed for the death of

Minos' son, and thus Athens must periodically pay tribute to Crete by sending fourteen youths and maidens to be imprisoned in the Labyrinth, perhaps starved in it, or eaten by the half-bull, half-man Minotaur. The Cretan Labyrinth containing the monster becomes *Dream*'s forest-maze, as in Titania's references in the play to 'the quaint mazes in the wanton green' or 'the mazed world' (2.1.99, 113). In Shakespeare's play, only four young people go there, and decidedly not to be sacrificed to a monster Minotaur but rather to court and woo. The playwright's Minotaur, to be sure, is the 'translated' Bottom, desired himself for a time by the fairy queen Titania. The mythic reference here is to Pasiphae's lust for the beautiful bull that results in her Minotaur offspring.[10] Like Pasiphae in Ovid's *Art of Love*, Titania is concerned about her would-be lover's food.[11] Thus, rather than devouring young people, Shakespeare's ass-head monster Bottom is hungry for 'a peck of provender,' 'your good dry oats' or 'a handful or two of dried peas' (4.1.31, 32, 37–38). Indeed, in *Dream* he never even meets up with the lovers in the woods.

Bottom's name ties in with the Theseus myth in that it refers to the 'bottom' or spool around which thread is wound,[12] and alludes to Ariadne's strategy for Theseus finding his way out of the Labyrinth. Shakespeare, the son of a so-called 'brogger' or unlicensed wool dealer, would surely be familiar with this meaning. Theseus' womanizing ways are recalled as well in Helena's name. An episode in the Theseus legend concerns the thirteen-year-old Helen, later of Troy, whom the fifty-year-old Greek hero kidnapped, 'ravished,' and wished to marry when she grew up (North 43–44).

Beyond the name allusions, other play details, too, recall the Theseus legend. Once again there is reference to the hero's famous philandering. In *Dream* Oberon accuses Titania of being party to Theseus' affairs with Perigouna [Perigenia], Aegles, Arieadne and Antiopa (2.1.74–80), a shortened catalogue of the mythic Theseus' many women. Theseus seduces Perigouna, after he defeats her murderous father. He promises to marry Ariadne, Minos and Pasiphae's daughter, when she provides Theseus with the strategy for defeating the Minotaur, but according to most accounts he abandons her and later marries her sister Phaedra. He also has relationships with Aegles and Antiopa, among others (North 41).

In the play, Shakespeare makes reference to Theseus driving out the Centaurs from the wedding feast of Pirathous and Hippodamia when Revels' Master Philostrate's list of entertainments includes 'The battle with the Centaurs, to be sung / By an Athenian eunuch to the harp' (5.1.44–45). This episode concerns the nuptials of Theseus' friend King Pirithous of Lipathae. The Centaurs, relatives of the bride, get drunk and attempt to rape the women of the wedding party, and one Centaur even tries to carry off the bride! Theseus defeats him, and subsequently helps drive all the Centaurs from the king's land.

Theseus' heroic model is his cousin and friend Hercules, with whom Hippolyta, as she reports in the play, once hunted (4.1.112). The duke also refers to 'my kinsman Hercules' (5.1.47), and Bottom brags to his fellows that he 'could play Ercles rarely.' After his 'audition' speech, he comments, 'This is Ercles' vein, a tyrant's vein' (1.2.29–40).

Because *Dream* is a comedy Shakespeare leaves out the more tragic episodes of the Theseus legend, such as accounts of Aegeus' and Hippolytus' deaths.[13] Theseus' character in *Dream* is mostly a composite of Chaucer's positive and rational 'duc ... Of Atthenes' in 'The Knight's Tale,' returned from war with the conquered Amazon queen 'Ypolita,' and Plutarch's portrait of Theseus as founder of the Athenian commonwealth and a populist, with something of Ovid's 'most valiant Prince.' Mowat points out that in weighing details from various sources, 'Plutarch ... represents himself as being almost in despair of giving "Theseus" a coherent "Life" [because] At every point in Plutarch's "Life of Theseus" are irreconcilable stories' (336).

Additionally, there is also the implicit dark side to the Greek hero. D'Orsay Pearson reminds us, 'the image of Theseus available to the Renaissance was hardly one of total reason and honor,'[14] that Shakespeare's audience would know that behind the pomp and ceremony of *Dream*'s Athenian court celebrating Theseus' wedding day are the hero's tragic miscues. Subtle hints at Theseus' moral inconsistency can be noticed in Shakespeare's plot. For instance, at the play's start, the duke tells Hermia he must uphold the law – 'fit your fancies to your father's will; / Or else the law of Athens yields you up / (*Which by no means we may extenuate* [emphasis mine]) / To death, or to a vow of single life' (1.1.118–21) – but later he changes his mind and overrules Egeus' appeal to the law: 'Egeus, I will overbear your will' (4.1.179). Though he would now wed Hippolyta, his line '[I] won thy love doing thee injuries' (1.1.17) may suggest rape. There is irony in Oberon's blessing at the end, that the 'issue' the three couples will create 'Ever shall be fortunate' (5.1.401–22), because an educated audience would know Theseus' marriage to Hippolyta produced Hippolytus, who was killed by his father. Similarly, Oberon's earlier prophecy in the play that Theseus and Hippolyta (and the other two sets of lovers) will enter a 'league whose date till death shall never end' (3.2.373) turns out to be false, according to the Theseus myth, just as the 'everlasting bond of fellowship' (1.1.85) the duke pledges for his marriage at the start of the play.

The various social classes represented by three of the groups in the play may have been prompted by Theseus' organization of the commonwealth of Athens. North writes: Theseus united the 'whole province of Attica ... promising [Athens] should be a commonwealth and not subject to the power of any sole prince but rather a popular state' (32–33). He continues, 'For he first divided the noblemen from husbandmen and artificers. ... And as the noblemen did pass the other in honor, even so the artificers exceeded them in number, and the husbandmen them in profit' (35). Bottom's gang, thus, could be identified with the 'artificers,' Egeus and the lovers the 'husbandmen,' and Theseus and Hippolyta the 'nobles.' Shakespeare creates distinct social classes in his comedy, with the god-like fairies overseeing and influencing the mortal world.

Several key aspects of Shakespeare's Theseus narrative ask for elaboration as they relate to themes in *A Midsummer Night's Dream*. These include the playwright's comic Minotaur installed in his woodland Labyrinth. In the myth the Minotaur's youthful prey are sometimes viewed as sexual sacrifices. Shakespeare glances at the lusty bull-monster when Flute laments his friend as 'sweet *bully* Bottom' (emphasis mine, 4.2.19). However, Bottom's ass' head seems less sexually toned than a bull's might be, despite Jan Kott's assertion (without supporting evidence) that 'From antiquity up to the Renaissance the ass was credited with the strongest sexual potency and among all quadrupeds was supposed to have the longest and hardest phallus.'[15] Yet Bottom's transformed 'nole' also could be taken as an asexual mule's head, pointing to Bottom's seeming lack of interest in sex with Titania; he is more interested in eating. Indeed, at one point Titania sends a 'venturous fairy' to fetch Bottom 'new nuts' (4.1.35–36). Bottom is not only the foolish monster in the maze, but also, with his down-to-earth literalness and exuberance, the way out of the labyrinth of the woodland world. Lamb notes that 'Bottom is an ass because he does not succumb to love; and he is a thread out of this labyrinth because he refuses to abandon his common sense even in Titania's embrace' (481).

Mowat sees Bottom's transformation as a subtle reference to Ovid's Actaeon changed to a stag (341), ironic in that Bottom seems so disinterested in sex. She notes that Ovid refers to Diana as 'Titania,' and Actaeon's hounds, like Theseus', 'are of "Crete" and "Sparta"' (341). However, as Freake contends, 'in relation to Titania Bottom seems like an indulged baby, child rather than consort of a mother goddess' (266). The fairy queen is the protective and nurturing mother to child-like Bottom. Along these lines, *Dream* can be seen as a play about gender conflict and patriarchal and matriarchal conflict for the control of children. Egeus tries to control Hermia's choice of husband, Oberon wants Titania's changeling boy, and Puck acts like Oberon's unruly and mischievous child. Oberon defeats Hippolyta with his sword and gets his boy while Hermia outwits her father and is coupled with her true love Lysander, and Helena gets her love Demetrius.

On Titania's mind is the moon weeping, 'Lamenting some enforced chastity' (3.1.200). Brooks interprets this line to mean that the moon weeps because chastity is 'violated by force' (62n.), but 'enforced chastity' could be read also as the moon weeping because there is no sex. The weaver's observation that he is 'marvail's hairy about the face' (4.1.24–25) might be Shakespeare recalling an incident from an early part of North's Theseus story about the shaving habits of the warriors of Abantes and the Macedonians (unlike the passive Bottom, they shaved heads and beards in order not to provide a hand-hold for their enemies), or, more likely, an off-color reference to pubic hair, since a 'bottom' (rear end) is 'up' (Bottom sports an ass' head) in *Dream*'s topsy-turvy world. The weaver exclaims, 'I am such a tender ass' (4.1.25). Indeed, Wall's 'lime and hair' and 'plaster,' 'loam,' 'roughcast' and '*stones*,' taken together, suggest male genitals treated for venereal disease, and Wall's '*crannied hole, or chink*' the posterior orifice (3.1.68–69; 5.1.181, 190–91). The joke is continued when Flute as Thisbe exclaims: '*I kiss the wall's hole, not your lips at all*' (5.1.201), likely an intended obscene stage direction.

Be that as it may, ass' ears as well point to Midas, who drank bull's blood when the Cimmerians, associated with darkness and sleep,[16] overthrew his kingdom. Midas earns his ears when he stupidly prefers Pan's music to Apollo's and doesn't anticipate the implications of his golden touch. Bottom, unlike Midas, tries to look ahead. He fears 'the [audience] ladies [for his play *Pyramus and Thisbe*] cannot abide' stage killing, and therefore a Prologue must explain: 'Pyramus is not kill'd indeed; ... tell them that I Pyramus am not Pyramus, but Bottom the weaver' (3.1.11–12, 19–21). He would have Snug acting Lion 'name his name' (3.1.36). During the *Pyramus and Thisbe* play, he steps out of his role several times.

Bottom is a child-like literalist whose dramatic dabbling lacks the golden touch of talent. Just as a willful child, he wants to play all the character parts.

Bottom and his gang have English Christian names and tags, rather than the to-be-expected classical names in Shakespeare's Athens. Nick Bottom might be seen as weaving cloth for Starveling the tailor, perhaps a costume maker. Along these lines, Snug the joiner (whose lion costume could have been prompted by Hercules' lion skin [see North 13]) might construct props (Quince says, 'I will draw a bill of properties, such as our play wants' [1.2.105–06]), Flute provide music along with tinker percussionist Snout, and Quince would write and/or direct the production – or perhaps be the theater architect, as 'quoin' has meaning as 'a wedge-shaped piece of stone or wood, also used to describe a cornerstone.'[17] Thus, the rude mechanicals are not only actors, but comprise an entire early-modern theater company! We see them cast, anticipate problems with the theatrical illusion, worry about the color of Pyramus' beard and rehearse and perform a play.

The comic Minotaur Bottom is found only briefly in Shakespeare's woodland maze. Moreover, *Dream's* labyrinth does not function as a confining cage or prison for the monster or a structure for sacrifice as in the myth; rather, it represents freedom from restraint for the lovers and a place to exercise imagination for the mechanicals. If one views Theseus' court world as one of law, reason, and order, Oberon's forest yields the opposite – confusion, chaos and perhaps even sin. Michael Wood sees it as 'part of the pre-Reformation imagination. For the Protestants, fairies, like ghosts, had been devised by popish priests from an earlier era to "keep the ignorant in awe."'[18] Lamb views the labyrinth as allegorically representing 'vice, especially yielding to sensual delights, in which sinners lose themselves until aided by some external power' (470). Ormerod states it this way: Shakespeare's labyrinth 'is an icon of blinded wrong choice, ... and it is also the process by which this moral confusion is transcended as the spiraling movements of the conventional emblematic labyrinth yield to the harmonious circles of the conventional concluding dance' (49).

The playwright takes his audience from the comfortable familiar to the imagined or dream-like, then back again. We begin with an ordered ducal court. A civilized wedding is in the offing. Then, moving from this socially cultured world to the world of the forest around Athens, passionate animal instincts and emotional disorder progressively come to the fore. Egeus' favorite Demetrius has rejected his former girlfriend Helena, who nonetheless spaniel-like still fawns on and abjectly follows him into the woods. She has told Demetrius of Hermia and Lysander's elopement. Lysander responds to Hermia's good advice to 'teach our trial patience' (1.1.152), with, first, his reasonable 'A good persuasion' (1.1.156), but, next, his sudden and irrational plan to run away to his 'widow aunt' (1.1.157). The lovers never find this aunt and perhaps she doesn't exist, for in the forest Lysander is intending to sleep with Hermia: 'One turf shall serve as pillow for us both, / One heart, one bed, two bosoms, and one troth' (2.2.41–42). To be sure, Hermia refuses, turning down her over-eager lover. Her strong-willed and passionate character, however, comes through mostly in her dealings with Helena, whom she accuses, when Puck mixes up affections, of stealing her man. Helena says of Hermia that 'though she be but little, she is fierce' (3.2.325).

In the forest, Shakespeare emphasizes that 'reason and love keep little company together now-a-days' (3.1.143–44). Titania loves the part-ass Bottom, and Lysander wakes to shift his affection from Hermia to Helena with the ironic appeal to reason:

> The will of man is by his *reason* sway'd;
> And *reason* says you are the worthier maid.
> Things growing are not ripe until their season,
> So I, being young, till now ripe not to *reason*;
> And touching now the point of human skill,
> *Reason* becomes the marshal to my will. (italics mine, 2.2.115–20)

Also confused in the woods is who chases whom. Helena points out as she pursues Demetrius that 'Apollo flies, and Daphne hold the chase; / The dove pursues the griffin; the mild hind / Makes speed to catch the tiger' (2.1.231–33). She continues, 'We [women] cannot fight for love, as men may do. / We should be woo'd, and were not made to woo' (2.1.241–42).

Just as things in the forest are turned upside-down for the lovers, they are also confused for the mechanicals. Their imaginations are stretched to the limit as they contemplate how to present moonshine or wall, or how their acting will affect their audience. When Snout declares, 'O Bottom, thou art changed!' (3.1.114), he is not critiquing the weaver in his role as Pyramus, for Bottom is in fact 'changed.' And Bottom's response to his colleague not only answers him, but underlines the function of satire for an audience: 'You see an ass-head of your own, do you?' (3.1.116–17). 'Lord, what fools these mortals be!' says Puck (3.2.115).

When Oberon states 'I am invisible' (2.1.186), he blatantly appeals to the audience's imagination. Theseus underlines the importance of audience imagination toward the end of *Dream* in his dialogue with Hippolyta: 'If we imagine no worse of them [the actors, in this case Bottom and his crew] than they of themselves, they may pass for excellent men' (see 5.1.215–16). The fairy forest world of Oberon, Titania and Puck asks us to take an especially imaginative leap. Shakespeare's benevolent, and sometimes mischievous, fairies seem to come from Shakespeare's fertile imagination rather than a specific source, and serve to identify a spirit, dream or forest world beyond the human but heavily involved in it. That is to say, with the fairies we are taken beyond the more familiar, to a world where perhaps tiny creatures (Oberon is a 'dwarf' in the source work *Huon of Burdeux*) control mortals in the manner of Greek or Roman gods.

These creatures fight over little things, exhibit the petty jealousies, just as mortals and the gods do. For Oberon and Titania it is an Indian 'changeling boy.' Thus, in our love story, we move from a father wishing to control a daughter, to lovers' elopement and cavorting in the woods, to imminent marriages, but also to the bickering of the seeming long 'married,' represented by Oberon and Titania. Further, perhaps the *Pyramus and Thisbe* play also suggests the tragic vicissitudes often associated with love.

It would be a mistake to make too much of Shakespeare's *structural* labyrinth in *Dream*. True, he has four interrelated groups of characters and therefore plots contained in his five-act structure, with Bottom as the comic 'Minotaur' in the dead center of his dramatic maze (3.1.102sd). Is Shakespeare, then, our Theseus leading his audience of sacrificial 'youths and maidens' into his labyrinth to meet the Minotaur? Rather, I think, the play is Shakespeare's reflexive exercise, taking us from the familiar into the dark forest of comic midsummer dreams and imagination, finally returning us to our usual selves by way of Puck's 'Epilogue.' At the end, Puck speaks directly to the audience and apologizes for the journey Shakespeare has taken us on, asking the audience to think of the play as a harmless midsummer night's dream:

> If we shadows have offended,
> Think but this, and all is mended,
> That you have but slumb'red here
> While these visions did appear.
> And this weak and idle theme,
> No more yielding but a dream,

Gentles do not reprehend.
If you pardon, we will mend.
And, as I am an honest Puck,
If we have unearned luck
Now to scape the serpent's tongue,
We will make amends ere long;
Else the Puck a liar call. (5.1.423–35)

Just as Bottom performs a 'Bergomask dance' at the conclusion of the *Pyramus and Thisbe* play, Theseus in the myth, too, does a dance after defeating the Minotaur: 'Then with the other young boys that he had delivered, he danced a dance, which the Delians keep to this day, as they say, in which there are many turns and returns, much after the turnings of the Labyrinth' (North 29).

Chapter 5
Richard III: *the dragon and Saint George*

The Theseus narrative is a combination of myth and fanciful quasi-history. So too is the English national myth that forms a background intertext to Shakespeare's *Richard III*. Despite the Reformation, images of Saint George and the Dragon were still commonplace in Protestant England. The boy Shakespeare, who likely came into the world on Saint George's day, might have been told about one such image on the west wall of the Stratford-upon-Avon Guild Chapel, whitewashed over just before he was born on order of his Borough Chamberlain father because it was thought to be too Catholic (Figure 5).[1] However, Shakespeare probably witnessed during his youth the popular yearly Pageant of Saint George and the Dragon that took place on Holy Thursday on the streets of Stratford-upon-Avon.[2] Saint George's slaying of the monster dragon can be seen not only as paralleling Theseus' defeat of the monster Minotaur, but also, with Shakespeare's *Richard III* in mind, Theseus' defeat of the Calydonian boar, another familiar legend.

Shakespeare's Richard III exhorts his troops before the battle of Bosworth Field with a war cry that crescendos to the paradoxical, 'fair Saint George, / Inspire us with the spleen of fiery dragons!' (5.3.349–50). *Richard III*, like Book 1 of *The Faerie Queene*, plays on the legend of Saint George and the Dragon, but unlike the focus of Edmund Spenser's narrative Shakespeare chooses to tell the dragon's story. The playwright makes Richard into the monster who ultimately will be vanquished by Richmond, Shakespeare's Saint George. Richard's war cry appeals to the patron of England, but his wish is ironically and significantly to fight like a dragon.

The first three books of *The Faerie Queene* were published in 1590 and *Richard III* came shortly thereafter – that is, in the period between 1591 and 1593.[3] A. Kent Hieatt writes that 'near the beginning of his career Shakespeare surely read with absorption *The Faerie Queene* 1590 (I–III),'[4] and a number of scholars have found Spenser's influence in Shakespeare's plays. E.M.W. Tillyard, for

Figure 5. *St. George and the Dragon*. Painting on the wall of the Chapel of the Trinity, Guild of Holy Cross, at Stratford-upon-Avon. By Permission of the Folger Shakespeare Library.

example, observes that especially in language the playwright seems 'to have learnt and applied the lessons of Spenser,'[5] and Wolfgang Clemen notes a Spenser-like simile in *Titus Andronicus*.[6] Judith H. Anderson argues that *The Faerie Queene* was 'demonstrably on Shakespeare's mind when he wrote *King Lear*,'[7] and she also finds allusions to Spenser's 'Garden of Adonis' in some of *Richard III's* imagery.[8] Harold F. Brooks, too, cites similarities with the 'Cave of Mammon' episode in Clarence's dream sequence.[9] However, despite two book-length studies of Shakespeare and Spenser, one by W.B.C. Watkins[10] and the other by Abbie Findlay Potts,[11] no one has noticed Shakespeare's likely debt in *Richard III* to the Saint George and the Dragon legend, conceivably suggested by the first book of *The Faerie Queene* and perhaps other works as well.

Spenser's main source for his Saint George story was *Legenda Aurea*, the thirteenth-century volume by Jacobus de Voraigne, Archbishop of Genoa, translated by William Caxton as *The Golden Legend or Lives of the Saints* (c. 1487).[12] By the time de Voraigne wrote down his hagiography it had become conflated with the Perseus myth (retold in Ovid's *Metamorphoses*), emphasizing not the saint's martyrdom but the hero's supposed encounter with a dragon. Like Perseus, Saint George was said to have slain a monster to rescue a damsel in distress. In Perseus' case, the princess Andromeda is the woman; she is chained to a rock as an offering to a threatening sea-beast. Similarly, the saint bests a sea-dragon terrorizing the daughter of the king of Silene. Saint George's narrative begins with the dragon, who can only be appeased by the sacrifice of, first, two sheep, then later, a sheep and a man, and, finally, only 'children and young people' (127). When the lot falls to the king's daughter, the monarch initially resists his own edict, but then dresses his daughter as if for her wedding and leads 'her to the place where the dragon was' (127). As fate would have it, just at that moment, Saint George passes by and demands of 'the lady what she made there' and why she is weeping (127). Quickly grasping her dire situation the saint declares, 'I shall help thee in the name of Jesu Christ' (128). When the dragon comes forward to challenge the warrior-saint, George 'garnished him with the sign of the cross ... and smote him with his spear and hurt him sore' (128). Our hero then directs the princess to harness the dragon with her girdle and lead him into the city. After exacting a promise from the citizens to 'believe ... in God, Jesu Christ,' the saint cuts off the dragon's head and subsequently, we are told, 'fifteen thousand men' were baptized, not counting women and children (128).

The historical Saint George is a shadowy character. The only 'fact' that has come down to us is that he was martyred at Lydda (also known as Diospolis) in Palestine before the time of Constantine. From the fourth century onward, however, his legend became embellished with details of his soldierly exploits, association with the Urmiah Christian community, and his travel to Britain. In the Middle Ages, Saint George was credited with aiding the Normans at the 1089 Battle of Antioch, and somewhat later the Crusaders adopted the warrior tribune as their guardian. In 1344 Edward III further honored him as patron of England, and in 1349 as protector of the knightly Order of the Garter. Hugh MacLachlan points out that 'even with the rise of Protestant hostility to saint cults, George persisted in England; when other saints' days were removed from the calendar during the revisions of Henry VIII, his was kept.'[13]

The saint is the warrior hero of the Mummers folk plays.[14] Additionally, there are records of more formal dramas in 1456, 1511 and 1577 devoted to him.[15] Richard Johnson's *The Renowned History of the Savern* [sic] *Champions of Christendom* (first published 1596–97) also tells his story. In his account, Johnson adapts and freely elaborates materials from the *Legenda Aurea*, *The Faeirie Queene* and the verse romance *Sir Bevis of Hampton*.[16] Thus, Shakespeare may have received his Saint George story from any number of places, but Spenser was certainly at hand just at the right time to jog the playwright's muse.

Caroline Spurgeon's classic study of Shakespeare's imagery reminds us that 'In *Richard III* there is a very small but quite continuous and insistent animal symbolism, all centering on Richard and bringing out the quality of ruthless cruelty in his character as it strikes those who come into contact with him.'[17] The accumulation of animal imagery surrounding Richard, and the associated characteristics of those animals, both real and fabulous, are meant to suggest Richard as dragon. G. Wilson Knight states that 'It is the dragon with which he recognizes personal kinship. He is, in fact, himself the Dragon.'[18]

Spenser's dragon can be seen as the final embodiment of the accumulated evils the Red Cross Knight encounters on his journey to holiness. Major sins represented along his way would include hypocrisy (for example, Archimago and Duessa), irreligion (Error and Sanfoy), lawlessness (Sansloy), despair (Terwin, Trevisan and Despair) and pride (Lucifera and Orgoglio). Shakespeare's Richard is guilty of each of these sins. He is a 'dissembler' (1.2.184) who clothes his 'naked villainy / With odd old ends stol'n forth of holy writ' (1.3.335–36). He 'know'st nor law of God nor man' (1.2.70), and admits to 'despair' just before his final battle:

I shall despair; there is no creature loves me,
And if I die no soul will pity me.

And wherefore should they, since that I myself
Find in myself no pity to myself? (5.3.200–3)

Moreover, his pride is everywhere in evidence.

Shakespeare constructs his dragon mostly from imagistic descriptions in his play. First of all, Richard is ugly, a 'lump of foul deformity' (1.2.57). The villain's own testimony affirms his twisted body. He has been 'sent ... / Into this breathing world scarce half made up,' is 'rudely stamp'd, ... Deform'd, unfinish'd' (1.1.20–1). 'Sin, death, and hell have set their marks on him' (1.3.292), and 'his hell-govern'd arm' (1.2.67) 'Is like a blasted sapling, wither'd up' (3.4.69). Francis Bacon writes in his essay 'Of Deformity' (1597):

> Deformed persons are commonly even with nature; for as nature hath done ill by them, so do they by nature; being for the most part (as the Scripture saith) *void of natural affection*; and so they have revenge of nature. Certainly there is a consent, between the body and the mind; and where nature erreth in the one, she ventureth in the other.'[19]

Bacon goes on to say that 'all deformed persons, are extreme bold,' and that 'deformity, is an advantage to rising' in station (170–71). New Arden editor Antony Hammond observes, 'This is such a good description of Richard's behaviour that one wonders if he was in Bacon's mind as he penned it' (102).

But it is animal imagery that dominates. Spider and toad images reinforce the hunchback's misshapen person and venomous character. He is twice called a 'bottled spider' (1.3.241; 4.4.81), 'bottle' suggesting his deformity and/or poisonous evil, and 'spider' pointing to his devious web-spinning plots to kill off his family and any one else in his way to achieving the kingship. Toads, too, with no necks, could be perceived as having hunched backs like Richard, and some are also venomous.

A veritable bestiary of menacing and threatening animals, Richard is labeled 'tiger' once (2.4.50), and 'dog' five times. Richard is ruthless and aggressive, like the dogs used to attack the lugged bears at the Southwark bear-baitings. Indeed, he describes himself punningly as 'curtail'd' (1.1.18). Queen Margaret also refers to him bitterly as 'dog' (1.3.215), and in the same scene warns Buckingham to 'take heed of yonder dog! / Look when he fawns he bites; and when he bites, / His venom tooth will rankle to the death' (1.3.288–90). Margaret also chides the Duchess of York: 'From forth the kennel of thy womb hath crept / A hell-hound that doth hunt us all to death'

(4.4.47–48). Richard is 'That dog, that had his teeth before his eyes, ... [a] carnal cur [who] / Preys on the issue of his mother's body' (4.4.49, 56–57). When Richmond at last kills Richard, the Earl proclaims, 'the bloody dog is dead' (5.5.2).

Richard is also associated with the basilisk, a fabulous and dragon-like beast. The Greek *basiliskos* translates as 'little king,' and because of the creature's characteristic bright, crown-like mark it was regarded as the king of serpents. Pliny the Elder was first to describe the basilisk fully:

> The basilisk serpent ... is a native of the province of Cyrenaica, not more than 12 inches long, and adorned with a bright white marking on the head like a sort of diadem. It routs all snakes with its hiss, and does not move its body forward in manifold coils like the other snakes but advancing with its middle raised high. It kills bushes not only by its touch but also by its breath, scorches up grass and bursts rocks. Its effect on other animals is disastrous: it is believed that once one was killed with a spear by a man on horseback and the infection rising through the spear killed not only the rider but the horse. Yet to a creature so marvelous as this – indeed kings have often wished to see a specimen when safely dead – the venom of weasels is fatal.[20]

A twelfth-century bestiary notes: 'if it looks at a man, it destroys him,'[21] and Chaucer writes in 'The Parson's Tale' that what is constant about the 'basilicok' is 'the venym of his sighte' (l. 852).[22] Richard Gloucester, in *Henry VI, Part 3*, comments 'I'll slay more gazers than the basilisk' (3.2.187). And Lady Anne, in *Richard III*, wishes that she had basilisk eyes so that she might kill Richard with her gaze (1.2.150).

The basilisk received its alternate name 'cockatrice' in the Middle Ages because the creature was reputed to be hatched by a toad or snake from an irregular cock's egg.[23] The prophet Isaiah declares, 'out of the serpents roote shal come forthe a cockatrise, and the frute thereof *shallbe* a fyerie flying serpent' (14:29), and, recalling Richard, evil men 'trust in vaintie, & speake vaine things: thei conceive mischief, and bring forthe iniquitie. They hatche cockatrice egges, & weave the spiders webbe' (59.4–5).[24] Jeremiah also cites serpents and cockatrices as divine punishment: 'For beholde, I will send serpents, & cockatrices among you, which wil not be charmed, & they shal sting you, saith the Lord' (8.17). The skeptical Sir Thomas Browne, in the seventeenth century, argued the cockatrice was 'an "Hieroglyphicall fancy," but the Basilisk, though not born from a cock's egg and not incubated by a toad, did exist as a real serpent' (quoted in White 168n.). In any case, Shakespeare uses both basilisk and cockatrice designations – 'cockatrice' in *The Rape of Lucrece* (l. 540), *Romeo and Juliet* (3.2.47) and *Twelfth Night* (3.4.196). In *Richard III*, the Duchess of York laments: 'O my accursed womb, the bed of death! / A cockatrice hast thou hatch'd to the world, / Whose unavoided eye is murtherous' (4.1.53–55).

Richard's heraldic crest, the *blanc sanglier*, figures a white boar. The origin of this emblem may suggest an anagram of *Ebor* (bore) which is the designation for York.[25] In the scene where Hastings is sounded out about Richard as potential king (3.2), Shakespeare has the lord iterate Gloucester's association with his signature animal. He tells Lord Stanley's messenger that his master's bad dream about a 'boar … [who] rased off his helm' (3.2.10) is foolish:

> And for his dreams, I wonder he's so simple
> To trust the mock'ry of unquiet slumbers.
> To fly the boar before the boar pursues
> Were to incense the boar to follow us,
> And make pursuit where he did mean no chase.
> … the boar will use us kindly. (3.2.26–33)

A Latin bestiary notes, 'we get the name of … Wild Boar from its savagery' (White 76), and in *Timon of Athens* Alcibiades, like Richard, is 'a boar too savage, [who] doth root up / His country's peace' (5.1.165–66). The boar is fearsomely 'scythe-tusk'd' (*The Two Noble Kinsmen*, 1.1.79). Shakespeare paints his most vivid picture of the beast in *Venus and Adonis*:

> On his bow-back he hath a battle set
> Of bristly pikes that ever threat his foes,
> His eyes like glow-worms shine when he doth fret,
> His snout digs sepulchers where e'er he goes;
> > Being mov'd, he strikes, what e'er is in his way,
> > And whom he strikes his crooked tushes slay.
> His brawny sides, with hairy bristles armed,
> Are better proof than thy spear's point can enter;
> His short thick neck cannot be easily harmed;
> Being ireful, on the lion he will venter.
> > The thorny brambles and embracing bushes,
> > As fearful of him, part, through whom he rushes. (ll.
> > 619–30)

The boar's apparent invulnerability expressed in these lines reminds us of Spenser's seemingly impenetrable dragon: 'And over, all with brazen scales was armed / Like plated coat of steel, so couched near / That nought mote pierce, ne might his corse be harmed / With dint of sword nor push of pointed spear' (*FQ* Bk. 1, 11.9.1–4). The 'deadly boar' (4.5.2) Richard is feared by his victims when they are awake, but also in prophetic dreams (3.2.11). Queen Margaret slurs his emblem by calling the hunchback 'hedgehog,' and she curses him further as an 'elvish-mark'd, abortive, rooting hog' (1.3.227).

Richard's faithful companions are other animals – Catsby and Ratcliff. Edward Hall, one of Shakespeare's acknowledged sources, recounts the story of 'a poore gentlemen called Collyngborne' who wrote a verse about Richard and his cronies that called attention to their animal associations: 'The Rat [Ratcliff], the Catte [Catsby] and Lovell our dogge / Rule all Englande under the hogge.'[26] Hall reports wryly that Richard, 'This poeticall schoolemayster corrector of breves and longes, caused Collynborne to be abbreviated shorter by the hed, and too be devyded into foure quarters' (quoted in Bullough 285).

'The devil,' reports a twelfth-century bestiary, 'bears the similitude of a wolf: he who is always looking over the human race with his evil eye, and darkly prowling round the sheepfolds of the faithful so that he may affect and ruin their souls' (White 59). Richard is referred to as 'wolf' at 1.2.19 in the Folio version of *Richard III*, and at 4.4.23 as well. Richard is 'hell's black intelligencer' whose object is, like Satan's, 'to buy souls / And send them thither' (4.4.71–73). There are devil and hell references attached to Richard throughout the play. The diabolical hunchback has made England, 'this other Eden, demi-paradise' (*Richard II*, 2.1.42), 'happy earth, … [his] hell' (1.2.51). Elizabeth exhorts Dorset: 'If thou wilt outstrip death, go, cross the seas, / And live with Richmond, from the reach of hell' (4.1.41–42). Richard is called a 'son of hell' (1.3.229), a 'black magician,' 'Foul devil,' 'devilish slave,' 'dreadful minister of hell,' 'cacodemon' and so on. Lady Anne declares that he is 'unfit for any place, but hell' (1.2.109), and Queen Margaret exclaims, 'Sin, death, and hell have set their marks on him, / And all their ministers attend on him' (1.3.292–93).

The Saint George and the Dragon narrative is, to be sure, a typological story. It not only recalls the Perseus myth, but also suggests the defeat of Lucifer by Saint Michael during the War in Heaven:

And there was a battle in heaven: Michael & his Angels foght against the dragon, and the dragon foght & his Angels. But they prevailed not, nether was their place founde anie more in heaven. And the great dragon, that olde serpent, called the devil and Satan, was cast out, which deciveth all the worlde: he wasever cast into the earth, & his Angels were cast out with him. (Rev. 12:7–9)

Similarly, Saint George's hagiography evokes the defeat of the dragon of the Apocalypse by the warrior Jesus Christ. John writes:

And I sawe the beast, and the Kings of the earth, and their warriers gathered together to make battle against him, that sat on the horse & against his soldiers. But the beast was taken ... And the remnant were slayne with the sworde of him that sitteth upon the horse. (Rev. 19:19–21)

The further text is Revelations 20:2–3: 'And he toke the dragon that olde serpent, which is the devil and Satan, and he bounde him a thousand yeres, And cast him into the bottomless pit.' Thus Richmond's victory over Richard at Bosworth Field is Shakespeare's rendering of a familiar religious motif.

Further, it may recall a popular ballad and possible play written around the time of Shakespeare's *Richard III*. In 1592, an anonymous broadside appeared entitled *A pleasant songe of the valiant actes of Guy of Warwicke, to the tune of 'Was ever man soe tost in love.'* The ballad details the hero's rescue of a lion from a dragon's jaws (read, hero Richmond saves lion England from dragon Richard III) and the slaying of a boar in Windsor Forest, among other adventures.[27] 'Guy was not merely a good knight, the conqueror of treacherous Dukes, Saracens, wild boars, dragons, and giants; he was also [like Saint George] a national hero' (Crane 135). In fact, Guy was considered 'only a little below King Arthur in renown' (Crane 142). Richard Johnson's *Seven Champions of Christendom* identifies him as the eldest son of Saint George, and the saint's companion in some of his adventures. Since Guy was associated with Shakespeare's home shire of Warwick, the playwright undoubtedly knew his legend. He may even have been distantly related to the local hero (Wood 44). Indeed, Guy's supposed relics were kept and displayed locally – his sword in Warwick Castle – and many considered his exploits as fact and not fiction.

Additionally, Alfred Harbage postulates that the play *Guy of Warwick*, printed in 1661, was actually written in 1593, that is, about the time of *Richard III*, and that Shakespeare is attacked in it in the guise of the clown Sparrow from Stratford-upon-Avon.[28] Indeed, some of the drama's language that Harbage does not note reminds us of *Richard III*. For example, the play contains a reference to 'Hell-hound' (Act II) and Time delivers the following lines: 'think then with apprehensive eyes you see / this warlike Lord [Guy of Warwick] boldly attempt to fight / with that fell savage Bore of Calledon / that spoiles the fields and murders passangers / him his sword subdu'd.' These may recall Richmond's lines, 'The wretched, bloody, and usurping boar, / That spoil'd your summer fields and fruitful vines, / Swills your warm blood like wash and makes his trough / In your embowell'd bosoms' (5.2.7–10). In addition to *The Faerie Queene* then, Guy of Warwick may also have been on Shakespeare's mind when he was writing *Richard III*.

Richmond appears for the first time in Act 5, scene 2, and he is painted the hero in bold strokes.[29] His language, and the language of his followers, is in marked contrast to that of Richard and his supporters. Saint-like Richmond continually invokes 'God' and asks Him to 'Make us thy ministers of chastisement' (5.3.113). He tells his soldiers that 'The prayers of holy saints and wronged souls, / Like high-rear'd bulwarks, stand before our faces' (5.3.241–42), and that Richard is 'God's enemy' (5.3.252, 253). Richmond appeals to 'God and Saint George' at the end of his stirring oration to his troops (5.3.270). The Earl's given name is Henry and not George, but the name George does figure symbolically in *Richard III*, first in the defeat of Clarence by Gloucester and finally in the salvation of Stanley's son by Richmond. Clarence, whose given name is George, is sent to the Tower because of 'a prophecy, which says that G / Of Edward's heirs the murtherer shall be' (1.1.39–40). The king has been told 'that by G / His issue disinherited should be' (56–57). But of course Richard's title, Gloucester, also begins with the significant letter, and further, if we think of Richmond as a symbolic Saint George he does ultimately 'disinherit' the Yorks to begin the Tudor line. Another George, the hostage young George Stanley, is saved despite being threatened by Richard if his father fails in his loyalty to the king (5.3.60–63). Richmond calls attention to young Stanley by asking just before the end of the play if this significantly named character is rescued.

As in the Mummers plays, the motif of Shakespeare's drama is archetypal. Spring and fertility will follow winter. The exiled hero from across the sea returns to his homeland now barren because the boar-dragon has laid waste to the land. The destructive beast has brought winter and sterility, and now must be purged for the earth to become fertile again. The play begins with seasonal imagery in Richard's first speech. It isn't winter yet – Gloucester's 'season' for battle and mischief – because of brother Edward's peaceful 'glorious summer' (1.1.2). Thus, Gloucester announces his intention to 'prove a villain' (1.1.30), and sets about to kill off his family and anyone else in the way of his becoming king.

Joseph Campbell's words about the archetypal villain suggest King Richard's character and black humor: 'The tyrant is proud, and therein resides his doom. He is proud because he thinks of his strength as his own; thus he is in the clown role, as a mistaker of shadow for substance.'[30] This 'bloody tyrant and a homicide' (5.3.246) is sacrificed for the good of the land. The battle takes place in the mythic center of the universe. Campbell again: 'The place of the hero's birth [to] ... which he returns to perform his adult deeds among men is the mid-point or navel of the world' (334). Indeed, Richmond locates Richard, 'this foul swine, / ... even in the centry of this isle [England]' (5.2.10–11). According to Campbell, 'the mythological hero is the champion not of things become but of things becoming; the dragon to be slain by him is precisely the monster of the status quo, ... the keeper of the past. From obscurity the hero emerges, but the enemy is great and conspicuous in the seat of power; he is enemy, dragon, tyrant.' (337).

Ultimately, Saint George-Richmond defeats the boar-dragon Richard, and thus expiates the sinful Lancastrian usurpation and murder of King Richard II. Richmond's successful victory over Richard metaphorically represents Christ's rescue of mankind from death and establishes the New Jerusalem.

At play's end Richard is in the role of a sacrificial scapegoat in accord with the Tudor myth. Tillyard reminds us, 'That a character should shift from a credible human being to a symbol would not have troubled a generation nurtured on Spenser' (242). Richard's person embodies the Plantagenet crimes that began with the deposition and regicide of Richard II, and included the ensuing evils connected with the War of the Roses and the Hunchback's personal sins during his rise to kingship. Richard is responsible for killing off most of the remaining Lancastrians and Yorkists. When he is wooed to the throne in a scene stage-managed by Buckingham, he is positioned between two clergymen. The audience recognizes the inversion of the tableaux of Christ between thieves. Richard is thus seen as the anti-Christ. Anthony Hammond notes:

Richard's is the one act of sacrifice needed to redeem England from her accumulated sins ... it restores England to grace. The anti-Christ takes the sins of the world on his shoulders not for altruistic, but for selfish reasons; he does not offer himself as ransom, but is pushed, fighting and shouting, to his fate. (107)

Unlike the regicide that murdered Richard II, Richard III's killing at Bosworth is understood as not a sin but as a necessary step toward the establishment of the Tudor 'golden age.' The uniting of 'the White Rose and the Red' (5.5.19) by Richmond and Elizabeth brings fertility again to the land: 'O now let Richmond and Elizabeth, / The true succeeders of each royal house, / By God's fair ordinance conjoin together! / And let their heirs (God, if thy will be so) / Enrich the time to come with smooth-fac'd peace, / With smiling plenty, and fair prosperous days!' (5.5.29–34).

We began by calling attention to Richard's paradoxical battle cry linking Saint George and dragon. There is a similar, though implicit, paradox for Richmond. While his 'oration to his soldiers' concludes with 'God and Saint George! Richmond and victory!' (5.3.270), with no mention of 'dragon,' one of his battle standards displayed on historic Bosworth Field figured the image of the Red Dragon of Wales. That is, Henry Tudor's ensigns not only carried banners representing Saint George, but also one with a 'Red ffyry dragon peyntid upon white and Grene Sarcenet.' Did Shakespeare intend the irony that the defeat of one dragon means replacement by another?

Chapter 6
Iago, James VI and the succession

Othello's third Arden editor E.A.J. Honigmann, challenging New Arden editor M.R. Ridley and others' 1604 dating of *Othello*, makes a convincing case for an earlier date, one when Queen Elizabeth was still alive.[1] Citing Philemon Holland's translation of Pliny's *Historie of the World* (1601) (which 'almost certainly supplied Shakespeare with much of the play's "foreign" and "exotic" material'); *Hamlet's* Quarto 1 echoes (published in 1603, but written earlier); *Twelfth Night's* casting similarities (including a boy actor who could sing) and relationships to other contemporary plays, Honigmann builds a substantial argument for his view. Furthermore, two other probable sources for *Othello* that Shakespeare likely consulted, Lewis Lewkenor's *The Commonwealth and Government of Venice* and *A Geographical Historie of Africa*, were published in 1599 and 1600 respectively, closer to Holland's Pliny and the composition of *Hamlet* and *Twelfth Night* than the traditional dating of *Othello*. Moreover, in 1600 the Moorish ambassador from the King of Barbary visited Elizabeth's court and had his now often-reproduced picture painted. It is even conceivable that Shakespeare met this exotic man, as the playwright's acting company performed at court during the 1600 Christmas season.[2] This chapter further supports Honigmann's early dating of *Othello* by linking Shakespeare's tragedy with the ongoing underground discussion in England and elsewhere concerning Scottish James' succession to the English throne.

I wish to suggest that the playwright's villain Iago is meant to be identified with King James VI of Scotland, a party to the failed Essex rebellion of 1601. James was to be the beneficiary of the coup d'état, or so he was led to believe by Robert Devereux and his supporters, who included Lord Strange, Samuel Daniel, John Harrington, and the Countess of Pembroke, all of whom Shakespeare most likely knew. Essex's good friend the Earl of Southampton, Shakespeare's patron, was also a party to the plot, and for his involvement was condemned to life imprisonment in the Tower (and only released when the new king took the throne). Essex's followers Sir Charles Percy, Sir Gelly Meyricke and others arranged a *Richard II* revival by the Lord Chamberlain's Men at the Globe Theater showing the deposition of a monarch, a scene left out of all printed versions of the play during Elizabeth's lifetime.[3] At Essex's trial for 'high Treason,' the actor Augustine Phillips, testifying as a witness, complained that his company did not want to perform Shakespeare's play, 'holdyng that play of Kyng Richard to be so old & so long out of vse as that they shold have small or no Company at yt.'[4] However, Sir Gelly Meyricke offered the company forty shillings to stage it, and Essex was reported to have 'greeted [it] with great applause giving countenance and lyking to the same' (Chambers 323). Even beyond the royal deposition scene, there are other possible identifications of King Richard with Queen Elizabeth regarding taxation policies, the difficulty of a ruler without an heir and, most of all, the Irish problem. In any case, the aging Elizabeth famously told a visitor to her Privie Chamber at East Greenwich that 'I am Richard the Second, know ye not that?' (Chambers 326). After Essex's trial and execution, Shakespeare and his company probably needed to demonstrate that he and it were in the queen's camp. A volume of verses that included Shakespeare's poem 'The Phoenix and the Turtle' alludes to Sir John Salisbury, who was knighted in 1601 for helping to suppress the Essex rebellion (Ackroyd 399). *Othello*, too, might have been part of an effort to celebrate Elizabeth's victory over dangerous rivals, and reprimand the Scottish James for his involvement in the scheme to supplant the queen. Shakespeare may have written *Othello* in part as an atonement for being a part – albeit an indirect part – of the Essex plot. My theory hinges on the identification of Iago with James, whose Christian name, foreignness, reputed vulgarity, attitude toward women, homosexuality and blatant ambition link him with Shakespeare's character. This kind of oblique attack on the Scottish king would not have been unique. In 1596, for example, James complained bitterly to Queen Elizabeth (by way of William Cecil, Lord Burghley) about Edmund Spenser's allegorical treatment of his mother, and, thus by implication, himself in Canto ix of Book V of *The Faerie Queene*.[5] The trial of Duessa before Mercilla (stanzas 28–50) was a transparent reference to Mary Queen of Scots' trial in 1587 and, in turn, an attack on James' right to the crown.[6] The king demanded of Elizabeth, 'that Edward Spencer [sic] for his faulte, may be duly tried and punished.'[7] Barbara Parker argues that Shakespeare's *Titus Andronicus* shows the playwright's 'antipathy to the succession of James.'[8] Her provocative reading associates Tamora Queen of Goths with Mary Queen of Scots and Aaron the Moor with Spain (see 110–129). Peter Ackroyd acknowledges that

Shakespeare wrote plays about contemporary situations, suggesting for example that '*Othello* was a very modern drama, reflecting all the circumstances of that period' (428). Under the direction of the Master of the Revels, drama was often used for propaganda purposes and to forward government policy. Ackroyd points out, although 'we can never hope to recover the full range of allusions that Shakespeare introduced within his drama, ... it is important to realize that they are nonetheless imbedded in his texts' (173).

Various rare early-Modern documents about who should succeed Elizabeth have been brought together by Jean-Christophe Mayer. Mayer titles his book *Breaking the Silence on the Succession*, calling attention to the official censorship of public discussion concerning Elizabeth's heir – the so-called 'Statute of Silence' – as promoted by the queen herself.[9] Swiss physician Thomas Platter, who visited England in 1599, reported that execution was the punishment for making inquiries about the succession.[10] Elizabeth, to be sure, was naturally loath to encourage succession talk for fear of compromising her power and opening destructive jockeying for preference, to say nothing of encouraging plots against her. However, her statute could not eliminate clandestine conversations about so important a subject; too much was at stake. By the mid-1590s there were at least ten (and maybe as many as fourteen) prospective candidates for the English throne, including Arabella Stuart, King Philip II of Spain, his daughter the Infanta Isabella Clara Eugenia, as well as James of Scotland (Mayer 3). Arabella Stuart, a first cousin of James, was descended from the queen's aunt Margaret Tudor and had been raised in England, considered by some supporters a distinct advantage. Phillip II, a descendent of Edward III and John of Gaunt, and his daughter Isabella were favored by Catholic interests. Marie Axton explains, 'In despair and with dubious legality ... Mary [Queen of Scots before her execution] had finally offered her claim and commended the Catholic cause to Philip of Spain.'[11] The Spanish king's candidacy, however, offered an interesting if scandalous parallel with the plot of Shakespeare's *Othello*. According to Ackroyd, there was 'a well-attested story published throughout Europe that the ... king of Spain, Philip II, was an insanely jealous husband who had strangled his wife in her bed. What is more, he had become suspicious of her when she had inadvertently dropped her handkerchief' (427). The protestant James' candidacy had another weighty problem: the Bond of Association (1584) and subsequent parliamentary legislation condemning his mother technically barred him from succeeding Elizabeth (Mayer 9–10).

Breaking the Silence on the Succession reprints a number of manuscripts and clandestinely printed documents from the period roughly between 1587 and 1603. Mayer points out that there was 'a sense of confusion [in the air,] largely because polemicists and ideologues could not agree on a definite rule of monarchical succession' (4). And this confusion, of course, was in large part complicated by religious issues. Who, for example, had the right to choose the next monarch – Parliament (under Henry VIII's dictates in his 1546 will), the Pope (as England's feudal overlord) or the reigning queen? Three years after her coronation in 1558 Elizabeth declared, 'when I am dead they shall succeed that have the most right' (quoted in Mayer 1). But who was this to be, and how was he or she to be chosen? Henry VIII's will decrees that descendents of his *younger* sister Mary, the Suffolk line, should succeed him, thus eliminating older sister Margaret's Stuart descendents. This dictate, to be sure, compromised the traditional notion of primogeniture, in turn barring Mary Queen of Scots and her son James from the English throne (Shapiro 113–14). A 1596 chapter added to the polemical *A Conference about the Next Succession to the Crowne of England* (1594) by N. Doleman (pseudonym of the Jesuit Robert Parsons) argued that the Pope had the right to choose. On the other side, Peter Wentworth, in *A Pithie Exhortation ... to Her Majestie ...* (1598) countered that the queen should submit her selection to Parliament for debate. Thomas Wilson, too, in an unpublished tract titled 'The State of England' (1600) writes that a monarch has 'no authority to ... dispose of the crown; that must be done by the general consent of all in Parliament. Yea, the king's eldest son, though the kingdom be hereditary, shall not be crowned without the consent of the Parliament after the death of his father' (quoted in Shapiro 139). The political in-fighting about who was to choose was meant obviously to favor or eliminate one candidate or another. And since laws and official policy squelched overt propagandizing, succession literature went underground in manuscripts, pamphlets, and allegorical works. Axton notes, 'the London Theatre of the late eighties and nineties perhaps [became] the freest forum for speculation about the future succession to the throne' (81).The Catholic Thomas Lodge, whose drama *The Wounds of Civil War* was performed by the Lord Admiral's Men in the mid- to late 1580s and published in 1594, titled his play to indicate what might happen in England if the succession was not resolved properly.[12] Parker's readings of *The Rape of Lucrese* and *Julius Caesar*, in addition to her previously mentioned *Titus Andronicus*, demonstrate Shakespeare's involvement in the succession question (see Parker 110–30, 31–54, 74–92). Similarly, *Julius Caesar* was not entered into the Stationer's Register in 1599 probably because it was considered dangerous for a play to show the assassination of a monarch (see Ackroyd 388). Shapiro, too, for example, notes the 'inpolitic' reference to the 'Scot ... [as] a giddy neighbor to us' in *Henry V* (1.2.144–45) (95). I believe that in *Othello*, too, Shakespeare set himself the difficult task of attacking James' candidacy at a propitious and critical moment (1601–2) hoping to mold public opinion, but at the same time disguising his insult well enough to have a strong alibi if he got into trouble.[13] A play with a Venetian setting and a plot based closely on an Italian novella, to say nothing of the Philip II story, provided just such cover. Richard Hillman notes, 'It is surely the key to much of the political meaning-making, in the drama of the period ... that the most radical suggestions become possible precisely because of their presumed, or at least presumable, remoteness from reality' (*Struggle* 317–18). Shakespeare's initial audience was the general public. Later, when *The Moor of Venice* by 'Shaxberd' was presented before King James in the Banqueting House at Whitehall on November 1, 1604, the question of succession was moot. Thus, the sitting monarch would have no reason to now recognize himself in the ambitious and crude soldier Iago. But perhaps in 1601 or 1602 people interested in the succession might have made the connection. Stephen Orgel points out that 'performances in the period were characteristically fluid.'[14] Citing the differing details of the *Macbeth* and *Winter's Tale* that Simon Forman saw as compared with the texts we have of these plays (see 32ff), Orgel also quotes the introductory epistle to the Beaumont and Fletcher Folio (1647): 'actors varied their performance according to their sense of the audience. ... The play before the king was not the same as the play at the Globe' (21).

Giraldi Cinthio, in the *Hecatommithi* source (1565) for *Othello*, does not name his villain; rather, he is merely designated *Alfieri*, 'Ensign.' Desdemona is the only named character in the novella, and following this lead Shakespeare gives his other characters Italian names to go with his Venetian setting. There is at least one glaring exception.[15] The name that he chooses for his villain is the Spanish 'Iago,' instead of the to-be-expected Italian 'Giaccomo.' Either designation is, of course, the equivalent of the English 'James' from the Latin *Jacobus*.[16] The superstitious king comments on his Christian name in a 1608 letter to Robert Cecil: 'the name given me of James included a prophetical mystery of my fortune, for as a Jacob I wrestled with my arms upon 5 of August for my life, and overcame [a reference to the Gowrie Plot[17]]; upon the 5 of November I wrestled and overcame with my wit [a reference to the Gunpowder Plot].'[18] What the king doesn't mention is that the etymology of his name suggests 'the supplanter,' referring to the Jacob and Esau narrative in Genesis 27.36 (Withycombe 161).[19] Barbara Everett argues correctly, Shakespeare was 'not going to donate that ... King's name to a villain without noticing what he is doing.'[20] She continues, '"Iago" was of all names the most recognizable both as Spanish and James' (103). Thus, this Spanish nomenclature represents a negative tag for the ensign and, in turn, the Scottish king. Spain was, after all, England's threatening enemy during the late sixteenth and first years of the seventeenth centuries, and supporter of Catholic Mary of Scots claim during Elizabeth's reign. Furthermore, the name 'Iago' recalls the patron saint of Spain, and the Spanish war cry that English sailors would have heard at various armadas, not only the famous one.[21]

Spain was, of course, Catholic, and James' religious sympathies were promoted as suspect by those who opposed him as England's next ruler. As Parker points out,

> In 1589, he [as James VI] had aroused suspicion by his lenient treatment of two Roman Catholic earls who, the English government discovered, had been in contact with Spain. In 1592, these same earls were implicated in the matter of the 'Spanish Blanks,' a secret plan for Spain's invasion of England. James, it was suspected, not only knew of the plan but was considering converting to Catholicism ['for a kingdom he will become a counterfeit Catholic' (quoted in Shapiro 140)] and enlisting Spanish aid himself in order to press his claim to the English crown. (Parker 115)

Mayer reports that in the late 1590s the rumor was that 'the king was ... favorably inclined towards the church of Rome' (*Breaking* 17), or, again, that he might possibly convert (*Breaking* 18). James was baptized in a Catholic rite, and Mary hoped that her son would become Catholic.[22] Richard Hillman writes that 'James never really stopped playing the catholic card dealt to him by his heritage.'[23] His early friend and intimate, the politically powerful Esmé Stuart d'Aubigny, whom the king created first Earl of Lennox (in 1580), and then the sole Duke of Scotland (1581), was a French Catholic agent before his conversion, perhaps motivated by expediency, to Protestantism. James' wife, Anne of Denmark, converted the other way, and she was sympathetic to peace with Spain.[24] The Venetian ambassador to England reported that 'The Queen ... became a Catholic owing to three Scottish Jesuits, one of whom came from Rome, the others from Spain' (Barroll 169). In a letter to the English Catholic Earl of Northumberland, James writes: 'As for the Catholics, I will neither persecute any that will be quiet and give but an outward obedience to the law, neither will I spare to advance any of them that will by good service worthily deserve it' (quoted in Willson 148–49).

When James was a teenager he wrote the long narrative poem *Lepanto*, probably in 1585 or a few year later, celebrating the Catholic victory over the Ottoman Turks at the Battle of Lepanto (1571).[25] By the 1590s, James' poem had been often reprinted and was widely known, also appearing in several translations. Pope Pius V had organized Catholic naval forces to fight the Turks over Venetian interests in Cyprus. Emrys Jones sees a connection between Lepanto, this last great galley's battle, and Shakespeare's *Othello*.[26] He, like others, assumes the tragedy was written in 1604 as a compliment to the new king of England, though he admits 'Shakespeare seems to have no direct indebtedness to James' (52). If I am correct that *Othello* was written before James came down to England, the tragedy's Lepanto connection might have been a *negative* reminder about James' 'Catholic' poem, thus constituting yet another item to stall the Scottish king's English candidacy. Willson cites the accusation that James had celebrated 'a Catholic triumph and [wrote] ... in praise of the Catholic commander, Don John of Austria' (66). Don John, illegitimate son of the Holy Roman Emperor Charles V, was the half-brother of Phillip II of Spain, and was mentioned as a possible husband for James' mother. He was also active in trying to free the imprisoned Queen Mary.[27] James' 'Apologie' to the reader that prefaces his *Lepanto*, included in *His Majexties Poeticall Exercises at Vacant Houres* (1591), attempts to answer Protestant critics of the poem. He writes: 'my invocation [is] to the true God only, and not to all the He and She Saints, for whose vaine honors, Don-Joan fought in all his wars.'[28] James continues, 'what so ever praise I have given to DON-JOAN in this Poeme, it is neither in accompting him as first or second cause of that victorie, but only as of a particular man.'

Shakespeare's tragedy *Othello* is obviously not centrally about religious issues; rather, it concerns, among other subjects, cultural themes. Cassio is characterized as a debonair, sophisticated and smooth-talking Florentine and Othello is a straight-forward, naive and innocent Moor. The general mistakenly enlists the supposedly

Venetian Iago to interpret local manners and women for him because Othello is an outsider. But Iago is also of foreign extraction, if we consider his Spanish name. And so too, really was the Scottish James. As Mayer remarks, 'the Scottish king was impeded [from England's kingship] by the fact that he was an alien and that, from a common law point of view, aliens could not inherit English land' (*Breaking* 15). James had a heavy Scottish accent, crude manners and a sexist attitude toward women that must have seemed very foreign and unrefined to Elizabeth's English court, and these features mirror Shakespeare's ensign's vulgarity.

The Scottish king's bawdy language, bad manners and unfashionableness were often remarked. One M. Fontenay, brother of Mary's French secretary, had this to say after observing the Scottish king: 'In speaking and eating, in his dress and in his sports, in his conversation in the presence of women, his manners are crude and uncivil and display a lack of proper instruction. He ... walks constantly up and down, though his gait is erratic and wandering. ... His voice is loud' (quoted in Willson 53). Later, when James was England's king, the French ambassador Beaumont wrote of him: 'He piques himself ... on great contempt for women. They are obliged to kneel before him when they are presented, he exhorts them openly to virtue, and scoffs with great levity at men who pay them honour' (quoted in Willson 196). James' poem 'A Satire against Woemen' suggests that 'all wemen are of nature vaine / And can not keepe no secret unrevealed,' hold grudges, are ambitious and crafty, and can't help following their nature (*Selected Writings* 139–40). Reports suggest that James' personal habits were repulsive; in an age when people bathed infrequently, apparently the Scottish king never even washed (Willson 379).

Similarly, Shakespeare characterizes his soldier Iago as lacking in refinement. According to a seventeenth-century second-hand source, 'the Person that Acted Iago [probably Robert Armin] was in much esteem for a Comoedian' (quoted in Chambers 261). The ensign's language is off-color. He shouts to Brabantio, 'an old black ram / Is tupping your white ewe' (1.1.87–88) and 'your daughter and the Moor are [now] making the beast with two backs' (1.1.115–17). Iago's aside referring to 'clyster-pipes' is especially vulgar (2.1.177). When the ensign concludes his diatribe about women (2.1.129–60), Cassio excuses his crude talk by remarking to Desdemona, 'You may relish him more in the soldier than in the scholar' (2.1.165–66).[29] Further, Iago's relationship with Emilia seems strained early in the play, and at the end Iago calls her a 'Villainous whore' (5.2.229) and stabs her. He promotes the false idea of Desdemona's infidelity, and even suggests the way to kill her: 'strangle her in her bed, even the bed she hath contaminated' (4.1.207–08). After Cassio is wounded by Iago, to divert attention from himself, he falsely implicates Bianca, calling her a 'strumpet' (5.1.117–23). Thus, Iago degrades all the women in the play. Indeed, he suggests that women are good only 'To suckle fools and chronicle small beer' (2.1.160).

Iago is also homosexual, albeit one that does not signal his sexual preference openly in the tragedy.[30] But the clues are there. Many have argued that hints in Shakespeare's drama point to this conclusion:[31] its setting in Venice ('home of the … homosexual');[32] Iago's figurative language, which is obsessively female and generative ('my Muse labors, / And thus she is deliver'd' [2.1.127–28]; 'There are many events in the womb of time which will be deliver'd' [1.3.369–70]; his plan 'is engend'red. Hell and night / Must bring this monstrous birth to the world's light' [1.3.403–04]), and especially his account of Cassio's supposedly erotic dream ('then [he would] kiss me hard, / … laid his leg / [Over] my thigh and [sigh'd], and [kiss'd]' [3.3.422–26]).

James' preference for young and handsome men throughout his life is both well known and well documented. It was even said in jest at the time that *King* Elizabeth was succeeded by *Queen* James. Sir John Oglander, knighted by James in 1615, writes: 'He loved young men, his favourites, better than women, loving them beyond the love of men to women. I never yet saw any fond husband make so much or so great dalliance over his beautiful spouse as I have seen King James over his favourites' (quoted in Bergeron 182). Early on, his relationship with his cousin Esmé Stuart, Duke of Lennox, caused him difficulty with the Scottish Kirk and nobles. Sir Henry Widdrington, in 1582, writes: 'The ministry are informed that the Duke [of Lennox] goes about to draw the King to carnal lust.'[33] After a meteoric rise to power engineered by James, Esmé Stuart was ultimately forced to leave Scotland and died in exile. James' poem *Phoenix*, published in his first volume of poetry, *The Essayes of a Prentise in the Divine Arte of Poesie* (1584), was a response to Lennox's death and a sort of allegorical elegy. The poem includes a prefatory acrostic verse, spelling out Stuart's name and 'DWIKE' {duke} in initial and final letters of each line.[34] David Bergeron argues that in *Phoenix* 'James voiced deep desire for his cousin, including homoerotic desire' (*Letters* 53). Bergeron continues:

> Everything in the poem speaks of the narrator's desire for the bird: its beauty, its soaring power, its brightness that rivals the sun, its attrac-

tiveness perceived by others, and finally its helplessness as it comes to seek refuge from attack. These same qualities James clearly found in Esmé. (*Letters* 60)

Bergeron notes, 'If the question is, did James and Lennox have a homosexual relationship, the answer is probably yes' (29). Willson, however, is unequivocal: 'His love for Lennox contained a sexual element' (36).

James' later lovers included Robert Carr and George Villiers. Like James, Carr had come to England from Scotland, gaining the king's attention in 1607 when he was thrown from his horse and broke his leg during an Accession Day tilt. Surviving letters from James to Carr, according to Bergeron, 'function as sites of homoerotic desire' (*Letters* 69). Just as in the case of Esmé Stuart's rise to power because of intimacy with the king, Carr also became a powerful intimate, and enjoyed favored status for a time. But his involvement in the murder of Sir Thomas Overbury resulted in his subsequent alienation from the king (see *Letters* 73–80).

James' last, and perhaps greatest, love was George Villiers, Duke of Buckingham. Buckingham's extensive correspondence with the king, according to Bergeron, 'reveals their intimacy and readily documents the homoerotic desire that permeated their relationship' (*Letters* 98). The following excerpt from a letter sent by James to Buckingham makes this unmistakably clear:

> we may make this Christmas a new marriage ever to be kept hereafter; for, God so love me, as I desire only to live in this world for your sake, and that I had rather live banished in any part of the earth with you than live a sorrowful widow's life without you. And so God bless you, my sweet child and wife, and grant that ye may ever be a comfort to your dear dad and husband. (Akrigg 431)

Ultimately, James was charged with sodomy with Buckingham, and his court was scandalously linked with that of Edward II (Bergeron 183), whose amours are well documented in Christopher Marlowe's *Edward II*.

James' homosexuality, foreignness, lack of refinement, attitude toward women and his given name with its Spanish Catholic associations together might suggest a portrait in Shakespeare's Iago, but it is the parallel of the ensign's ambition for the lieutenancy and the Scottish king's ambition to rule England that link them most securely. Iago is at first unsuccessful in his quest for promotion, despite enlisting 'Three great ones of the city, / In personal suit to make me his [Othello's] lieutenant, / ... I am worth no worse a place' (1.1.7–11). He argues jealously, suggesting James' primogeniture argument, 'Preferment goes by letter and affection, / And not by old gradation, where each second / Stood heir to th' first' (1.1.36–38). Iago finally achieves his goal by manipulating Othello and plotting against and discrediting Cassio.

Whenever possible and over a long period of time, the Scottish James unabashedly campaigned for the England kingship enlisting whomever he could. Willson notes, 'With all his soul he yearned for the English succession. He was ready to accept it, said a disillusioned Jesuit, from the Devil himself' (138). The first key to the succession was maintaining a good relationship with the English queen, which he tried to do even while his mother was alive. In the mid-1580s he wrote a sonnet for Elizabeth and sent it to her:

> Full many a time the archer slacks his bow
> That afterhend it may the stronger be.
> Full many a time in Vulcan'[s] burning stow
> The smith does water cast with careful ee.
> Full oft contentions great arise, we see,
> Betwixt the husband and his loving wife
> That sine they may the firmlyer agree
> When ended is that sudden choler strife.
> Yea, brethren, loving other as their life,
> Will have debates at certain times and hours.
> The winged boy dissentions hot and rife
> Twixt his lets fall like sudden summer showers.
> Even so this coldness did betwixt us fall
> To kindle our love as sure I hope it shall. (quoted in Akrigg 72)

Willson cites a letter suggesting 'that the King was prepared to sacrifice his mother if forced to choose between her and the English succession' (76). When Elizabeth had Mary executed in 1587, considering the gravity of the event, James protested very cautiously about his wounded honor. In a conciliatory letter, the Scottish king writes, 'I look that ye will give me at this time such a full satisfaction in all respects as shall be a mean to strengthen and unite this isle, establish and maintain the true religion, and oblige me to be, as of before I was, your most *loving and dearest brother*' (Akrigg 84–85). In 1596, James named his second child, and first daughter, after Elizabeth, and asked that she be her godmother. As much as possible, in most of his letters he was careful to keep on the good side of the English queen.

However, when it came to promoting his bid for the kingship he secretly supported the Essex rebellion. He directs his ambassadors at the English court in early February 1601 to follow 'the advice of my friends there,' meaning Essex and his associates, and just after the failed *coup* sent an obsequious letter to the queen speaking of 'great misunderstanding' and 'our constant amity' (Akrigg 169–70, 168). Akrigg notes, 'It is impossible to say how far James was party to the activities that culminated in the Essex Rebellion of 1601 (before his arrest Essex apparently destroyed incriminating letters from James), but [other letters] ... seem to indicate that James was deeply implicated' (9). John Bruce, however, asserts: 'It seems clear that Essex had been in correspondence with that sovereign [James VI] for a considerable time, certainly from the year 1598.'[35] Indeed, writes Bruce, 'He was infinitely grieved for the fate of Essex,' calling him 'his martyr' (xxix). However, after Devereux's trial and execution, this did not stop James, in the spring of 1601, from entering into a clandestine correspondence with Robert Cecil, because Essex's former enemy now supported James' ambition. Toward the end of Elizabeth's reign, James continually sent ambassadors to the queen's court on any excuse in order to discover the queen's health (was it failing?) and mind (would she favor him for the succession?).

I have argued here that Iago is a negative portrait of James VI, and thus Shakespeare writes against the Scottish king's succession. Ackroyd notes that 'the absence of Shakespeare from ... [the] cast-list of royal panegyrists [for the festivities associated with James' ascension] is somewhat puzzling' (425). Parker conjectures, however, that several of Shakespeare's later plays, after James has become England's king and Shakespeare's theater company patron, continue to criticize the now James I. In *Antony and Cleopatra* she sees a reflection of 'the infamous licentiousness and decadence of James and his court' in the behavior of the title characters (105). Further, she sees the play mirror 'James's neglect of statecraft for hunting' (105–06). Similarly, *Coriolanus*, she contends, reflects in part the contemporary power struggle between Parliament and Crown, with Martius as James disdaining the 'commons' and promoting his elitist Divine Right philosophy (54–57). Parker even argues, in an unpublished paper from a Shakespeare Association of America seminar (2004), that *Macbeth*, a play usually cited as complimentary to the king, 'presents the English-Renaissance stereotype of Scotland as a semi-barbaric realm ... [with] a nobility endemically prone to treason, and a topography enhancing the impression of a realm demonically possessed. There is also the Scots king, Macbeth himself; goaded by "Vaulting ambition" (1.7.27), he will stop at nothing to possess the crown.' Indeed, he murders a divinely appointed monarch.

The question, though, is what motive Shakespeare might have in slurring the now ensconced James? Perhaps popular drama could, with relative safety, criticize the ruler, his court and his policies. Perhaps, on the other hand, for the royal patron of Shakespeare's company, it was time for the playwright to be politic and celebrate him. Did Shakespeare find himself needing to compliment the king? James loved plays, and the dramatist apparently wrote his Scottish play *Macbeth* expressly for him. James traced his ancestry to Banquo, survived the Gunpowder Plot, cured the sick with a laying-on of hands, wrote a book on witchcraft, and, perhaps most of all, favored short plays![36]

Chapter 7
Shakespeare as his own prompt

Early in *Macbeth*, fulfilling the witches' prophesy, King Duncan honors Macbeth with the new title 'Thane of Cawdor,' and the surprised hero responds, 'why do you dress me / In borrowed robes?' (1.3.108–09). It is, of course, a given and no surprise that Shakespeare's plays are also 'dressed in borrowed robes,' in that they derive from many direct sources and a wide range of other intertextual prompts. We have noted some of them in this study. As we have observed, the playwright responded to sometimes subtle outside cues for his dramas, but he also returned often to settings, characters, names, stage business, and themes that had served him previously.

Some of his recycles are obvious, as for example his reuse of settings undoubtedly popular with his English audiences. Ancient Britain is where *Macbeth*, *King Lear* and much of *Cymbeline* take place, and a historically closer England for the ten early and late history plays. *Titus Andronicus'* Rome returns as a locale in the later tragedies *Julius Caesar, Antony and Cleopatra* and *Coriolanus*. Shakespeare likewise favored more modern Italy, thought of by the Elizabethan and Jacobean English as an exotic landscape where anything odd, horrible or exciting might happen, and the playwright sets seven of his plays there. *The Merchant of Venice's* city is reprised in the first act of *Othello*, *The Two Gentlemen of Verona* shares a Signory location with *Romeo and Juliet* and *The Taming of the Shrew's* Padua is also in this Venetian orbit. Other Italian settings are to be found in *Much Ado About Nothing* (Messina) and *All's Well That Ends Well* (Florence). Italian associations in an imagined land figure in the Illyria of *Twelfth Night* and *The Tempest* features characters from Milan and Naples. 'Green worlds' contrast with court worlds in various comedies, and the fantasy forest in *The Merry Wives of Windsor* harkens back to the enchanted woodland of *A Midsummer Night's Dream*. Pastoral landscapes occur in *As You Like It* and *The Winter's Tale*. The 'three houses' of classical comedy are suggested in the stage settings of, for example, *The Comedy of Errors* and *Twelfth Night*.

Another clear instance of Shakespeare's recycling involves characters. The playwright revived a number of early characters in more mature plays, at times modifying their characterizations in the newer context. The cowardly Sir John Falstaff of *Henry VI, Part 1* is amplified into the witty and engaging Falstaff of the two *Henry IV* plays, and the like-named but mostly transmogrified pudding guts and would-be seducer in *The Merry Wives of Windsor*. Sir John's fellows – Poins, Bardolph, Pistol, Peto, Nym, Mistress Quickly – appear variously in the comedy and the *Henry IV* and *V* plays, and in the hostess' case with varied designations. Justice Robert Shallow in *Henry IV, Part 2* reappears in Windsor. Prince Hal sheds his former mates and 'throw[s] off' his 'loose behavior' (*1Henry IV*, 1.2.208) in *Henry V*. Mark Antony in *Julius Caesar* becomes a title character and rather dissolute in *Antony and Cleopatra*. Shakespeare, a father of twins, has two sets of identical twins prompting the farcical fun in *The Comedy of Errors*, while the fraternal twins in *Twelfth Night* are written into a later romantic plot. Aaron the Moor anticipates the moor Othello, but still more the villainous characters Richard Gloucester, the bastard Edmund and especially Iago. Sir Toby Belch is a character cousin to Sir John Falstaff.

Shakespeare also reuses character names, for example Maria in both *Love's Labor's Lost* and *Twelfth Night*. Of the name 'Rosaline,' Romeo tells the Friar, 'I have forgot that name, and that name's woe' (2.3.46), but Shakespeare obviously didn't forget the name that he had used in *Love's Labor's Lost*. Julietta in *Measure for Measure* recalls the similarly named Juliet and Julia. The name Adriana, in *The Comedy of Errors*, is revived in its masculine form for a Volscian in *Coriolanus* and a lord in *The Tempest*. Antonios abound in the plays and Kate seems Shakespeare's favorite female name. The playwright is fond, too, of oxymoronic names (a common Christian name followed by a descriptive tag) for comic characters, as in Christopher Sly, Anthony Dull, Abraham Slender and Pompey Bum, to recall but a few.

The convention of all-male actors undoubtedly inspired the cross-dressing in comedies early and late. It occurs for the first time in *The Two Gentlemen of Verona* and the last in *Cymbeline* but is seen in middle plays, as Jessica, Portia, Nerissa, Rosalind, Celia and Viola don male attire in order to elope, function in a male world or avoid problems and dangers. Scholars have found homoeroticism in Shakespeare's sonnets, and with the Antonio characters in *The Merchant of Venice* and *Twelfth Night*, and later with Iago in *Othello*.

Sexual jealously is an obvious passion for the characters Othello, Posthumus Leonatus and Leontes, and just plain old jealousy for Don John.

Zany farcical madness constitutes stage business in *The Comedy of Errors*, and both feigned and 'real' madness occurs in *Titus Andronicus*, *Hamlet* and *King Lear*. Melancholia in varying degrees saddens the merchant Antonio, Portia, Don John, Jacques, Orsino, Timon and Pericles. Feste and Lear's Fool are melancholy as against their expected humor. Shakespeare's use of comic dialect promotes laughter in *Love's Labors Lost*, *The Merry Wives of Windsor* and *Henry V*.

One might include many other repeated devices and techniques, such as plays within plays (*A Midsummer Night's Dream*, *Hamlet* and *The Tempest*) and various types of prologues and epilogues. *The Taming of the Shrew* contains 'Induction' scenes, *Romeo and Juliet* a sonnet giving away the plot, *Henry IV, Part 2* and *Henry V* choruses, *Pericles* the poet John Gower, and *Troilus and Cressida* and *Henry VIII* unnamed prologue speakers. There are ten epilogues in the plays, among them Puck's, Rosalind's, Feste's, Pandarus' and Prospero's.

Ghosts and the supernatural were popular stage business with early English audiences, and Shakespeare employs these metaphysical effects prominently in a number of plays. So too was on-stage and reported violence, as in *Titus Andronicus* and *King Lear*. Sword fights are exciting action in the histories and tragedies, and comic fun is derived from proposed dueling that never materializes (as for instance between Sir Andrew and Viola, or Sir Hugh and Dr. Caius).

When Robert Armin joined the Lord Chamberlain's Men, there were more songs to be sung. 'When That I Was and a Little Tiny Boy,' is used in both *Twelfth Night* and *King Lear*. Rings constitute stage business in many plays, for example *The Two Gentlemen of Verona*, *The Merchant of Venice*, *Twelfth Night*, *All's Well That Ends Well* and *Cymbeline*. *All's Well* has a supposed substitute bride for a dead heroine as does *Much Ado About Nothing*. There are 'bed tricks' in two of the problem comedies. One could go on and on with numerous instances of clearly repeated themes, motifs, imagery and so on. Shakespeare recycled a lot! That said, I turn now to a subtle and more extensive self-borrowing, to my knowledge one that has been overlooked.

* * * *

The Taming of the Shrew and *All's Well That Ends Well* are rarely, if at all, thought of as related. Though both plays have been mentioned as possible candidates for the 'missing' *Love's Labor's Won*, referred to in Francis Meres' *Palladis Tamia: Wit's Treasury*, they seem worlds apart.[1] The former is a bright and sunny comic romp while the latter is a mostly sober and somewhat troubling mixed-genre play. Despite their stark tonal difference, however, the early comedy and the later problem play are nonetheless similarly indebted to popular folk material – *The Taming of the Shrew* to the familiar narrative about the reformation of a cursed and froward woman and *All's Well That Ends Well* to the tale of the 'clever wench' who accomplishes a 'miracle cure' and fulfills an 'impossible task' involving a 'bed trick.' Shakespeare also, it is clear, employed with gender variation *The Taming*'s plot outline for *All's Well That Ends Well*. The comedy presents Petruchio, who is determined to marry and tame the shrewish Katerina just as the problem play has Helena bent on wedding and reforming the headstrong and misguided Bertram.[2] Both Petruchio and Helena wish to improve their lot, the man by marrying a rich wife and thus adding to his estate and the woman by wedding an aristocratic count and bettering her social position.

Additionally, *The Taming of the Shrew* and *All's Well That Ends Well* are similar coming-of-age narratives, accounts of the lessoning and maturation of youthful characters. Kate is perhaps justifiably self-willed, feeling put upon by her father who views her as a disagreeable burden to marry off, and her favored sister, on the surface a maid of 'mild behavior and sobriety' (1.1.71). Kate's response is juvenile rebellion, striking out in tantrums and physically against what she takes to be her unfair, cruel and confining world. She is rude to everyone, ties up the hands of her sister (2.1.4) and presumably smashes a lute over Hortensio's head (see sd 2.1.141). Bertram is also decidedly immature. He is sent to the French court 'an unseason'd courtier' with LaFew to 'Advise him' (1.1.71, 72), but he has the misfortune to be 'misled ... [by the] snipt-taffata fellow' (4.5.1–2) Parolles, a 'counterfeit module' (4.3.99) whose 'soul ... is his clothes' (2.5.44). Paris and the court is the initial 'learning place' (1.1.177) for the young count. Despite the king's express command to marry his household servant Helena, Bertram refuses: 'A poor physician's daughter my wife! Distain / Rather corrupt me ever!' (2.3.115–16). Such willfulness, to be sure, incurs the monarch's anger – 'Proud, scornful boy, [you are] unworthy [of] this good gift' (2.3.151) – and Bertram learns that 'It is in ... [the king's power] to plant ... honor where / ... [he] please[s] to have it grow' (2.3.156–57). As a nobleman by birth he should obey the king, not only his feudal overlord but also his 'surrogate father' (1.1.7).

Signaling the plays' education themes, each drama has an Italian setting. Padua was a famous Renaissance university center, a 'nursery of arts' (*The Taming of the Shrew* 1.1.2), a place for 'learning and ingenious studies' (1.1.9).[3] Kate's education, however, does not take place in university lecture halls, but rather in harsh personal tutorials in or outside her home and at Petruchio's country house. Petruchio swears he will 'cuff' her if she strikes him (2.1.220), and he trains her as he might his falcons (4.1.197–209). He teaches by example; his behavior is even more perverse than hers to show her how her actions appear to others. Bertram's learning is of a different sort than Kate's. Florence, Machiavelli's city, is associated in *All's Well* with the Florentine wars. A French Lord declares these wars, 'well may serve / A nursery to our gentry' (1.2.15–16). But Bertram is told that he is presently 'Too young,' ''tis too early' and he must wait until 'the next year' (2.1.28) to become a soldier. One reason is that Florence contains an irresistible temptation – 'Those girls of Italy' (2.1.19) – for an immature young man. Nonetheless, following the bad counsel of his parasite Parolles, Bertram disobeys and departs Paris for Florence. Despite military success ('It is reported that he has taken their great'st commander, and that with his own hand he slew the Duke's brother' [3.5.5–7]), he succumbs to the charms of the Italian girl Diana and attempts to seduce her. Diana tells the young count that his duty is to his wife, and he also soon discovers that Parolles is as morally hollow as the drum that he claims he will rescue. The parasite is all words and no action, as indicated by his name.

Both plays begin with dead parents. Petruchio comes to Padua soon after his father's death (1.2.54), and similarly Helena reports that her father has died 'Some six months since' (1.2.71). Bertram's father, too, is also recently deceased, and the Countess wishes her son Bertram to 'succeed ... [his late] father / In manners as in shape!' (1.1.61–62). The French King also hopes that the young count will inherit his 'father's moral parts' (1.2.21) in addition to his physical features. Because we hear nothing of Kate's mother, we may assume that she is no longer alive. Just as Bertram suffers from a father's absence, Kate's aberrant behavior can also be seen as in part due to the lack of a mother figure.

Petruchio comes 'to wive it wealthily in Padua; / If wealthily, then happily in Padua' (1.2.75–76), and Helena aspires to happily marry her love, the aristocratic Count of Rossillion. She acknowledges, 'he is so above me' that there is 'ambition in my love' (1.1.87, 90). But why, Helena reasons, would the 'power [i.e., God] ... [that] mounts my love so high' (1.1.220) cause her to love Bertram without wishing her to act upon that love? Petruchio is confident that he can change Kate, and Helena likewise believes 'Our remedies oft in ourselves do lie' (1.1.216). Both are successful risk takers. With masculine bravado, Petruchio embarks on the seemingly impossible task of transforming Kate the shrew. His Herculean labor is to bring Katerina 'from a wild Kate to a Kate / Conformable as other household Kates' (2.1.277–78). Similarly, Helena's initial challenge – making the French king well – also seems impossible as the 'most learned doctors' (2.1.116) have already given him over. However, she is willing to put her life on the line with the king in order to win Bertram as a husband. Helena risks death 'With vildest torture' (2.1.174) if she does not succeed.

   The Taming of the Shrew and *All's Well That Ends Well* also involve unusual weddings and their aftermaths. With bluster and self-confidence Petruchio woos and wins Kate: 'And will you, nill you, I will marry you' (2.1.271). Likewise, with courage and determination Helena follows Bertram to Paris, cures the king and boldly asks for a husband of her choice. Her choice, of course, is Bertram. But the petulant count, after first refusing Helena and then reluctantly marrying her, declares, 'I will not bed her' (2.3.270). Moreover, he gives his new wife the impossible tasks of getting a ring from off his finger 'which [he declares] never shall come off,' and showing him 'a child begotten of thy body that ... [he is] father to' (3.2.57–59). Petruchio, in turn, arrives late for his wedding, is inappropriately dressed, and departs before the wedding supper. During the ceremony he swears ' "by gogs-wouns," ... / That all amaz'd the priest let fall the book, / And as he stoop'd again to take it up, / This mad-brain'd bridegroom took him such a cuff / That down fell priest and book, and book and priest' (3.2.160–64). Despite some earlier religious references associated with the king's cure (see 2.1.136–40), Helena can also be viewed as rather casual about religion in one instance. She blatantly lies about a pilgrimage to 'Saint Jaques' (3.4.4) in order to pursue her new husband to Florence.

   A climactic moment in Shakespeare's *The Taming of the Shrew* occurs when an exuberant Petruchio demands a public kiss from his transformed and obedient wife: 'Come on, and Kiss me, Kate' (5.2.180). Though not indicated in a stage direction, presumably he gets one. In contrast, a much quieter moment occurs in the 'problem play' when the newly married Helena modestly begs a private kiss from her husband: 'like a timorous thief, [she] most fain would steal / What law does vouch ... [her] own' (2.5.81–82). Helena voices her reluctant request to Bertram negatively: 'Strangers and foes do sunder and not kiss' (2.5.86). But she is denied her due.

On the other hand, Helena's pursuit and ultimate success in marrying and finally winning over Bertram may thematically suggest a loosening of the rigid paternalistic social structure seen in *The Taming of the Shrew*, where men seemingly rule the public, if not the private, roost. From this vantage, Helena can be seen as successfully challenging a class-conscious and male-dominated traditional society. She strikes out on her own, with the good offices and blessings of her 'surrogate mother' the Countess, and strives to marry above her station. Just as in *The Merry Wives of Windsor* with Anne Page and Fenton, Shakespeare suggests here the coming together of aristocratic name with bourgeois shrewdness and self-interest. Helena's and Bertram's child-to-be will engender noble blood and middle-class values.

Each play ends with the promise of new life. Helena is pregnant with Bertram's child and Petruchio exclaims, 'Come, Kate, we'll to bed' (5.2.184), suggesting future fruits of their marriage. The endings are also kinds of beginnings for the action the audience has just witnessed. Shakespeare suggests that the stories will be repeated again with other characters. Bianca and the Widow are recognized as shrewish women who must be tamed by their new husbands (Lucentio and Hortensio will attend Petruchio 'taming school' [see 4.2.54–58]). And, the King of France rewards the helpful Diana: 'Choose thou thy husband, and I'll pay thy dower' (5.3.328), just as he has allowed Helena to also choose an aristocratic husband and provided a dower for her.

Michael Wood has it right, then, when he describes Shakespeare as 'a magpie who borrowed or stole as much as he could decently get away with.'[4] As we point out in this final chapter, he even took a lot of material from himself!

Notes

Chapter 1

1 *All's Well That Ends Well*, 4.3.71. All references to the plays, unless otherwise noted, are quoted from *The Riverside Shakespeare*, second ed., G. Blakemore Evans et al., eds. Boston, MA: Houghton Mifflin, 1997.

2 Jeanine Parisier Plottel, 'Introduction'. *Intertextuality: New Perspectives in Criticism*. Eds Jeanine Parisier Plottel and Hanna Charney, *New York Literary Forum*, vol. 2, 1978, p. xiv. Plottel notes that this is her translation of 'tout texte se construit comme mosaïque de citations, tout texte est absorbtion et transformation d'un autre texte.' Julia Kristeva, *Séméotikè: Recherches pour une sémanalyse*. Paris: Editions du Seuil, 1969, p. 146.

3 *Image, Music, Text*. Stephen Heath, trans. New York: Hill and Wang, 1977, p. 159.

4 *Intertextuality*. London: Routledge, 2000, p. 1.

5 *Shakespearean Intertextuality: Studies in Selected Sources and Plays*. Westport, CT: Greenwood Press, 1998, p. 1.

6 *The Authentic Shakespeare*. New York: Routledge, 2002, p. 10.

7 'What is an Author?' In David Finkelstein and Alistair McCleery, eds. *The Book History Reader*. London: Routledge, 2002, pp. 225–30.

8 *Shakespeare: The Biography*. New York: Doubleday, 2005, p. 333.

9 See James Shapiro. *A Year in the Life of William Shakespeare, 1599*. New York: Harper Collins, 2005, p. 304.

10 New York: Oxford University Press, 1973.

11 See Allen, *Intertextuality*, pp. 140–41.

12 *Ruin the Sacred Truths: Poetry and Belief from the Bible to the Present*. Cambridge, MA: Harvard University Press, 1989, p. 53.

13 Geoffrey Bullough, ed. *Narrative and Dramatic Sources of Shakespeare*, 8 vols. London: Routledge, 1957–75. Kenneth Muir. *Sources of Shakespeare's Plays*. New Haven, CT: Yale University Press, 1977.

14 Oxford: Oxford University Press, 2000; in *Cambridge Companion to Shakespeare*, eds Margreta de Grazia and Stanley Wells. Cambridge: Cambridge University Press, 2001, pp. 31–47; London: Athlone, 2001.

15 *Shakespeare on Film*. Bloomington: Indiana University Press, 1977, p. 14.

16 *Shakespeare*. New York: Basic Books, 2003, p. 139.

17 Quoted in M.C. Bradbrook. *John Webster: Citizen and Dramatist.* New York: Columbia University Press, 1980, p. 21.

Chapter 2

1 All Marlowe references are to the following text: Sylvan Barnet, ed. *Doctor Faustus by Christopher Marlowe.* New York: New American Library, 1969. This is an edition based on the B text, but incorporating relevant A text passages. See pp. 103–09.

2 Fredson Bowers, ed. *The Complete Works of Christopher Marlowe.* Vol. 2. Cambridge: Cambridge University Press, 1973, p. 123.

3 See John Russell Brown, ed. *The Arden Shakespeare: The Merchant of Venice.* New York: Random House, 1964, p. xxxi, and Geoffrey Bullough, ed., *Narrative and Dramatic Sources of Shakespeare.* Vol. 1. London: Routledge and Kegan Paul, 1957, pp. 454–57.

4 *Shakespeare: The Biography.* New York: Doubleday, 2005, p. 147.

5 *Essays on Elizabethan Drama.* New York: Harcourt, Brace, and World, 1956, p. 56.

6 John Henry Jones, ed. *The English Faust Book.* Cambridge: Cambridge University Press, 1994.

7 See François Laroque, 'An Analogue and Possible Secondary Source to the Pound-of-Flesh Story in *The Merchant of Venice.*' *Notes and Queries* (New Series) 30 (April 1983), pp. 117–18.

8 One wonders here if there isn't some comic circumcision allusion, as this Jewish ritual fascinated early modern England. See Murray J. Levith. *Shakespeare's Italian Settings and Plays.* London: Macmillan, 1989, p. 28.

9 See Richard Horwich, 'Riddle and Dilemma in *The Merchant of Venice.*' *Studies in English Literature* 17 (1977), pp. 191–200.

10 'Biblical Allusion and Allegory in *The Merchant of Venice*'. *Shakespeare Quarterly* 13 (1962), p. 337.

11 Although Antonio also remains unmarried, he is understood to be the saintly, Christ-like Christian, as we shall see below.

12 But, as Dr. Johnson points out, Shakespeare seems to have forgotten this condition at 2.9.70 (Brown, p. 67n.).

13 See Murray J. Levith. *What's in Shakespeare's Names.* Hamden, CT: Archon, 1978, pp. 79, 89. Cynthia Lewis, in *Particular Saints: Shakespeare's Four Antonios, Their Contexts, and Their Plays*, Newark: University of Delaware Press, 1997, suggests that *Bastinao*, close to *Bassanio*, is an Italian diminutive for Sebastian, and might suggest that Bassanio is meant to be associated with the saint, p. 28.

14 *Geneva Bible: A Facsimile of the 1560 Edition*. Madison: University of Wisconsin Press, 1969. All biblical references are to this text.

15 To be sure, some critics, and especially Romantic writers like Goethe, see a sub-text here: Faustus as the Renaissance man of integrity and courage who makes a tragic but ultimately heroic choice.

16 Antonio's name recalls two important saints, Saint Anthony the Great (also known as Saint Anthony of Egypt, Saint Anthony the Hermit, and Saint Anthony Abbot) and Saint Anthony of Padua, both models of Christian forbearance. Saint Anthony the Great lived from 250–356 CE, and his reputation came to the West during the time of the Crusades (see Saint Athanasius, *The Life of St. Anthony the Great*. Willits, CA: Eastern Orthodox Books, 1970, pp. 5–50). One of the frequently rendered subjects in Medieval and Renaissance art, this Saint Anthony is remembered as an acetic who distributed his wealth among the poor and struggled against and resisted various evil demons. His 'Life' contains a sermon on temptation (pp. 15–29). Among his own temptations is an instance of silver and gold placed in his path by the devil, but Saint Anthony ignored them. He is often pictured with a pig, symbolizing his triumph over gluttony and sensuality, and he is the patron of swineherds. A 'Tantony pig' is the smallest of a litter, a detail that might recall Antonio's description of himself in Shakespeare's play as the 'tainted wether of the flock' (4.1.114). Saint Anthony the Great is also remembered for combating heresy and offering himself as a victim for martyrdom, again similar to Antonio's role in Shakespeare's *Merchant* (see Lewis, pp. 45, 30, 53).

Saint Anthony of Padua, who lived a brief life from 1195 to 1231, is the patron of lost property, suggesting Bassanio's appeal to Antonio in the first scene of the play: 'In my school-days, when I had lost one shaft, / I shot his fellow of the self-same flight / The self-same way with more advised watch / To find the other forth, and by adventuring both / I oft found both' (1.1.140–44). This Saint Anthony is also the apostle of charity, invoked for both spiritual and temporal needs, and the patron of lovers and of marriage as well. Also to the point of *Merchant* is the episode in Saint Anthony's life of the heretic (in some versions Jewish) who refused to believe in the presence of Christ in the Eucharist unless his mule knelt before the Sacrament. This happened, and many were converted (see Mary Purcell. *St. Anthony and His Times*. Dublin: M.H. Gill, 1960, pp. 87–89, 112; and Lewis, pp. 17, 15).

17 *The Bottom Translation: Marlowe and Shakespeare and the Carnival Tradition*. Trans. Daniela Miedzyrzecka and Lillian Vallee. Evanston, IL: Northwestern University Press, 1987, p. 17.

18 'The Theology of Marlowe's *The Jew of Malta*.' *Journal of the Warburg and Courtauld Institute* 27 (1964), p. 214.

19 John D. Jump, ed. *The Revels Plays: Doctor Faustus by Christopher Marlowe*. London: Methuen, 1962, p. 48n.

20 *The Scholemaster*. Ed. Edward Arber. London: Constable, 1920, p. 83.

21 *Shakespeare and the Jews*. New York: Columbia University Press, 1996, p. 76.

22 The Papal Bull was titled *Regnans in Excelsis*. It was subsequently published in a translation by recusant William Allen in 1588 as Pope Sixtus V's *Declaration of the Sentence and Deposition of Elizabeth the Usurper and pretensed Queene of Englande*. See Catherine Lisak, ' "Succession" versus "Usurpation": Politics and Rhetoric in Shakespeare's *Richard II*.' In Jean-Christophe Mayer, ed. *The Struggle for the Succession in Late Elizabethan England*. Montpellier, France: Astraea Texts, 2004, pp. 353–69.

23 Paul Siegel, 'Shylock the Puritan.' *Columbia University Forum* 5 (Fall 1962), p. 15. Abbr. in text STP.

24 Paul Siegel, 'Shylock and the Puritan Usurers.' *Studies in Shakespeare*. In Arthur D. Matthews and Clark M. Emery, eds. Coral Gables, FL: University of Miami Press, 1953, p. 135. Abbr. in text SPU.

25 *The English Drama in the Age of Shakespeare*. Philadelphia, PA: Lippincott, 1916, p. 109.

26 A.H. Bullen, ed. *The Works of John Marston*. Vol. 3. London: John C. Nimmo, 1887, p. 271.

27 New York: Riverhead, 1998, p. 175.

28 *The Occult Philosophy in the Elizabethan Age*. London: Ark Paperbacks, 1983, p. 187.

29 *Forbidden Knowledge*. New York: St. Martin's, 1996, p. 80n.

Chapter 3

1 Betty Rose Nagle, trans. *Ovid's Fasti: Roman Holidays*. Bloomington: Indiana University Press, 1995, p. 171.

2 See Jonathan Bate. *Shakespeare and Ovid*. Oxford: Clarendon Press, 1994, pp. 25–32.

3 W.H.D. Rouse, ed. *Shakespeare's Ovid: Being Arthur Golding's Translation of the Metamorphoses*. Carbondale: Southern Illinois University Press, 1961, p. 2.

4 George Sandys. *Ovid's Metamorphosis Englished*. In *Mythologized and Represented in Figures*, Karl K. Hulley and Stanley T. Vandersall, eds. Lincoln: University of Nebraska Press, 1970, p. 295.

5 Robert Graves. *The Greek Myths*. Vol. 2. Harmondsworth: Penguin, 1955, p. 399.

6 'Titian and Marsyas.' In *FMR* 4 (1984), p. 64.

7 *Titian: The Flaying of Marsyas.* Trans. Till Gottheiner. London: Spring Books, 1962, p. 8.

8 See Murray J. Levith. *Shakespeare's Italian Settings and Plays.* London: Macmillan, 1989, pp. 30, 79–82.

9 David Howarth. *Lord Arundel and His Circle.* New Haven, CT: Yale University Press, 1985, p. 15.

10 Mary F.S. Hervey. *The Life and Correspondence of Thomas Howard, Earl of Arundel.* Cambridge: Cambridge University Press, 1921, p. 52.

11 See Lionel Cust and Mary F.S. Hervey. 'The Lumley Inventories' and 'A Lumley Inventory of 1609.' Oxford: Walpole Society, vol. 6, 1918, pp. 15–50.

12 See Pierre Rosenberg. 'The Flaying of Marsyas.' In *Titian: Prince of Painters.* Susanne Biadene and Mary Yakush, eds. New York: Prestel, 1990, p. 370.

13 John Tucker Murray. *English Dramatic Companies 1558–1642.* Vol. 1. New York: Russell and Russell, 1963, pp. 20–22.

14 John Tucker Murray. *English Dramatic Companies 1558–1642.* Vol. 2. New York: Russell and Russell, 1963, p. 322.

15 The youthful Henry Wriothesley, Shakespeare's eventual patron, replaced Philip Howard for a time as the hope of English Catholics, as the Earl of Southampton was baptized and raised a Catholic.

16 Robert M. Adams, ed. *Ben Jonson's Plays and Masques.* New York: Norton, 1979, p. 340.

17 *The Arden Shakespeare: Coriolanus.* London: Methuen, 1976, pp. 24–29. Chambers suggests 1608. *William Shakespeare: A Study of Facts and Problems.* Vol. 1. Oxford: Clarendon Press, 1930, p. 480.

18 'Realism and Classicism in the Representation of a Painful Scene: Titian's 'Flaying of Marsyas' in the Archiepiscopal Palace at Kromeriz.' In *Czechoslovakia Past and Present.* Vol. 2. Ed. Miloslav Rechcigl, Jr. The Hague: Mouton, 1968, p. 1391.

19 See George Ferguson on Saint Sebastian. In *Signs and Symbols in Christian Art.* New York: Oxford University Press, 1961, p. 142.

20 *Titian.* Vol. 3. London: Phaidson, p. 91.

21 London: Methuen, 1963, pp. xxi–xxiv.

22 *Giulio Romano.* Vol. 1, p. 193n.

23 This image, it has been argued, is not of Coriolanus but of Alexander the Great (see Janet Cox-Rearick, ed. *Giulio Romano: Master Designer.* New York: Hunter College, 1999, pp. 104–05); the Yale University Art Gallery has also titled the drawing 'Ordeal by Fire of Quintus Cincinnatus.'

24 New York: Scholars Facsimiles & Reprints, 1938, p. 281b.

25 Geoffrey Bullough, ed. *Narrative and Dramatic Sources of Shakespeare.*

Vol. 2. London: Routledge and Kegan Paul, 1958, pp. 16–18; John
M. Steadman, 'Falstaff as Actaeon: A Dramatic Emblem.' *Shakespeare
Quarterly* 14:3 (Summer 1963), p. 243.

26 *Shakespeare's English Comedy.* Lincoln: University of Nebraska Press,
1979, p. 75.

27 The 1602 Quarto passage can be found in the Third Arden, ed.
Giorgio Melchiori. Walton-on-Thames: Thomas Nelson, 2000, pp. 319,
316b.

28 Oxford: Clarendon Press, 1989, pp. 226–27.

29 The Third Arden reprints the entire 1602 Quarto version of *The
Merry Wives of Windsor* as an appendix, and Giorgio Melchiori argues that
this version is probably an acting version of the play.

30 See John Frederick Nims, ed. *Ovid's Metamorphoses: The Arthur
Golding Translation 1567.* Philadelphia, PA: Paul Dry Books, 2000,
pp. 67–69.

31 Roberts begins to recognize this motif when she writes: 'Rebirth and
baptisms – the expulsion from the buck basket and the dip in the Thames
– have failed. Physical punishment – the cudgeling by Ford – has failed.
Lest there be any doubt, we have Mistress Page's announcement that the
group's objective is to "dis-horne the spirit"' (4.4.64 [2188]).

Chapter 4

1 *The Oxford Shakespeare: The Merry Wives of Windsor.* Oxford: Clarendon
Press, 1989, p. 23.

2 G.K. Hunter. *John Lyly: The Humanist as Courtier.* Cambridge, MA:
Harvard University Press, 1962, p. 318.

3 *Narrative and Dramatic Sources of Shakespeare.* Vol. 1. London:
Routledge and Kegan Paul, 1957, pp. 367–422; *The Arden Shakespeare:
A Midsummer Night's Dream.* London: Methuen, 1979, pp. lviii–lxxxix.

4 *Shakespearean Intertextuality: Studies in Selected Sources and Plays.*
Westport, CT: Greenwood Press, 1998, pp. 4, 118.

5 '"A local habitation and a name": Shakespeare's Text as Construct.'
Style: vol. 23, No. 3 (Fall 1989), p. 336.

6 See Murray J. Levith. *What's in Shakespeare's Names.* Hamden, CT:
Archon, 1978, pp. 75–76; M.E. Lamb, '*A Midsummer-Night's Dream*:
The Myth of Theseus and the Minotaur.' *Texas Studies in Literature
and Language* 21:4 (Winter 1979), pp. 478–91; David Ormerod, '*A
Midsummer Night's Dream*: The Monster in the Labyrinth.' *Shakespeare
Studies* 11 (1978), pp. 39–52; Douglas Freake, '*A Midsummer Night's
Dream* as a Comic Version of the Theseus Myth,' in Dorothea Kehler,

ed. *A Midsummer Night's Dream: Critical Essays*. New York: Garland, 1998, pp. 259–74; Peter Holland, 'Theseus's Shadows in *A Midsummer Night's Dream*,' in Stephen Orgel and Sean Keilen, eds, *Shakespeare and the Literary Tradition*, New York: Garland, 1999, pp. 39–51.

7 See Thomas North, trans. *Plutarch's The Lives of the Noble Grecians and Romans*. Vol. 1. New York: The Heritage Press, 1941, pp. 36–37, 39.

8. F.N. Robinson, ed. *The Works of Geoffrey Chaucer*. Boston, MA: Houghton Mifflin, 1957, p. 44 (ll. 2837–38).

9 Hermia's name might have been suggested by North when he writes of 'the city of Hermionia' in his Plutarch translation of Theseus' life, p. 16.

10 See Lamb, p. 480, and Freake, p. 269.

11 As does Titania, she feeds him: 'she cut / Fresh, tender leaves and grass for him.' James Michie, trans. *Ovid: The Art of Love*. New York: Modern Library, 2002, p. 23.

12 The *OED* quotes Walter Raleigh's *The History of the World*: 'He [Theseus] received from her [Ariadne] a bottome of thred' (9254). See also Caxton's trans. of *Aeneid*. quoted in Holland, p. 149.

13 Aegeus commits suicide after Theseus fails to fly the white sail upon his return after slaying the Minotaur, and Hippolytus is killed by his father due to the false accusations of Theseus' then wife Phaedra.

14 ' "Unkinde" Theseus: A Study in Renaissance Mythography.' *English Literary Renaissance* 4:2 (Spring 1974), p. 278.

15 *Shakespeare Our Contemporary*, Boleslaw Taborski, trans. Garden City, NY: Anchor Books, 1966, p. 227.

16 See Golding's translation of *Ovid's Metamorphoses*. John Frederick Nims, ed. Philadelphia, PA: Paul Dry, 2000, p. 292. Book 11, lines 687–89.

17 *OED*, VIII, p. 76.

18 *Shakespeare*. New York: Basic Books, 2003, p. 49.

Chapter 5

1 See James Shapiro. *A Year in the Life of William Shakespeare, 1599*. New York: Harper Collins, 2005, pp. 148–49.

2 See Michael Wood. *Shakespeare*. New York: Basic Books, 2003, p. 55.

3 See Anthony Hammond, ed. *The Arden Shakespeare: King Richard III*. London: Methuen, 1981, p. 61; Stephen Greenblatt, et al., eds. *The Norton Shakespeare*. New York: Norton, 1997, p. 507; and G. Blakemore Evans, et al., eds. *The Riverside Shakespeare*, second ed. Boston, MA: Houghton Mifflin, 1997, p. 748.

4 'William Shakespeare,' in *The Spenser Encyclopedia*. Eds A.C. Hamilton et al. Toronto: University of Toronto Press, 1990, p. 641.

5 *Shakespeare's History Plays*. New York: Collier Books, 1962, p. 238.

6 *The Development of Shakespeare's Imagery*. New York: Hill and Wang, 1951, p. 23.

7 'The Conspiracy of Realism: Impasse and Vision in *King Lear*.' *Studies in Philology* 84 (Winter 1987), pp. 12–13.

8 *Biographical Truth: The Representation of Historical Persons in Tudor-Stuart Writing*. New Haven, CT: Yale University Press, 1984, pp. 118, 223–24ns.

9 'Clarence's Dream.' *Shakespeare Survey* 32 (1979), pp. 145–50.

10 *Shakespeare and Spenser*. Princeton, NJ: Princeton University Press, 1950.

11 *Shakespeare and The Faerie Queene*. Ithaca, NY: Cornell University Press, 1958.

12 Vol. 3. London: J.M. Dent, 1900, pp. 125–34. All quotations in this paragraph are from this Caxton-translated text.

13 'St. George,' in *The Spenser Encyclopedia*, pp. 329–30.

14 Saint George in these folk dramas defeats a dragon and/or a 'Turk' to suggest the defeat of winter by spring. See Alan Brody. *The English Mummers and Their Plays*. Philadelphia: University of Pennsylvania Press, 1969.

15 See Edwin Greenlaw, Charles G. Osgood and Frederick M. Padelford. *The Works of Edmund Spenser*. Vol. 1. Baltimore, MD: The Johns Hopkins University Press, 1932, p. 380; and F.P. Wilson. *The English Drama 1485–1585*. New York: Oxford University Press, 1969, p. 7.

16 See the modern edition: Richard Johnson. *The Seven Champions of Christendom (1596/97)*. Ed. Jennifer Fellows. Aldershot: Ashgate, 2003.

17 *Shakespeare's Imagery*. New York: Macmillan, 1935, p. 232.

18 *The Sovereign Flower*. London: Methuen, 1958, p. 23.

19 *The Essays*. Mount Vernon, NY: Peter Pauper Press, n.d., p. 170.

20 H. Racham, trans. *Pliny: Natural History*. Cambridge, MA: Harvard University Press, 1956, p. 57.

21 *The Book of Beasts*. T.H. White, trans. and ed. London: Jonathan Cape, 1954, p. 168.

22 *The Works of Geoffrey Chaucer*. F.N. Robinson, ed. Boston, MA: Houghton Mifflin, 1957, p. 256.

23 See Joseph Nigg, ed. *The Book of Fabulous Beasts*. New York: Oxford University Press, 1999, p. 580.

24 All biblical quotations are from the *Geneva Bible: A Facsimile of the 1560 Edition*. Madison: University of Wisconsin Press, 1969.

25 Paul Murray Kendall. *Richard the Third*. New York: Norton, 1956, p. 134.

26 Quoted in Geoffrey Bullough, ed. *Narrative and Dramatic Sources of Shakespeare*. Vol. 3. London: Routledge and Kegan Paul, 1960, p. 285.

27 R.S. Crane. 'The Vogue of *Guy of Warwick* from the Close of the Middle Ages to the Romantic Revival.' *PMLA* 30 (1915), p. 151.

28 'A Contemporary Attack on Shakespeare.' *Shakespeare Association Bulletin* 16 (1941), pp. 42–49. Michael Wood agrees, noting that 'sparrow' and 'spear' were close in pronunciation in Elizabethan English, and that the dig at Shakespeare was among others at this time (see Wood, p. 146).

29 The herald's notes included in the application for Shakespeare's coat of arms implies that an ancestor 'fought with Henry Tudor against Richard III at Bosworth in 1485' (see Wood, p. 19).

30 *The Hero With a Thousand Faces*. Cleveland, OH: Meridian Books, 1956, p. 337.

Chapter 6

1 See *The Arden Shakespeare: Othello*. Ed. M.R. Ridley. New York: Vintage, 1967, p. xv; and *The Arden Shakespeare: Othello*. Third ed. E.A.J. Honigmann, ed. Appendix 1, 'Date.' Walton-on-Thames: Thomas Nelson, 1997, pp. 344–50.

2 Peter Ackroyd. *Shakespeare: The Biography*. New York: Doubleday, 2005, p. 427.

3 Shakespeare had previously referred to Essex in laudatory terms in the Chorus to Act 5 of *Henry V* (ll. 29–34). Blair Worden argues that Shakespeare's *Richard II* is not the play performed at the Globe on February 7, 1601, but rather a dramatization of John Hayward's *The First Part of the Life and Reign of King Henry IV* (1599). See 'Which Play was Performed at the Globe Theatre on 7 February 1601,' *London Review of Books* 25:13 (July 10, 2003), pp. 22–24.

4 Quoted in E.K. Chambers. *William Shakespeare: A Study of Facts and Problems*. Vol. 2. Oxford: Clarendon Press, 1930, p. 325.

5 David M. Bergeron. *Royal Family, Royal Lovers: King James of England and Scotland*. Columbia: University of Missouri Press, 1991, pp. 45–46.

6 In addition to Queen Elizabeth herself as the dedicatee of *The Faerie Queene*, Lady Elizabeth Carey, wife of the Lord Chamberlain, patron of Shakespeare's company, also was honored with a commendatory sonnet.

7 James Emerson Phillips. *Images of a Queen: Mary Stuart in Sixteenth-Century Literature*. Berkeley: University of California Press, 1964, p. 202.

8 Barbara L. Parker. *Plato's Republic and Shakespeare's Rome: A Political*

Study of the Roman Works. Newark: University of Delaware Press, 2004, p. 136.

9 Montpellier, France: Astraea Texts, 2003, p. 8. Abbr. henceforth in text, *Breaking*.

10 See James Shapiro. *A Year in the Life of William Shakespeare, 1599*. New York: Harper Collins, 2005, pp. 139–40.

11 Marie Axton. *The Queen's Two Bodies: Drama and the Elizabethan Succession*. London: Royal Historical Society, 1977, p. 76.

12 See Charles Whitworth, 'Thomas Lodge, *The Wounds of Civil War* and the Elizabethan Succession Crisis,' in Jean-Christophe Mayer, ed. *The Struggle for the Succession in Late Elizabethan England*. Montpellier, France: Astraea Texts, 2004, pp. 299–311. Abbr. henceforth in text, *Struggle*.

13 Apparently Shakespeare was not blamed or punished for the *Richard II* revival, and Southampton and Percy had relatively lenient sentences for their involvement. James' name was kept out of the Essex trials altogether, probably by Robert Cecil.

14 *The Authentic Shakespeare*. New York: Routledge, 2002, p. 240.

15 Actually two. The other is 'Roderigo,' which was the Christian general's name in the Battle of Clavijo (see next note).

16 See E.G. Withycombe. *The Oxford Dictionary of English Christian Names*. London: Oxford University Press, 1973, pp. 163–64.

17 A mysterious event aimed at discrediting the Duke of Lennox, and driving a wedge between him and James. It involved detaining the king, and resulted in the deaths of the Master of Ruthven and the Earl of Gowrie, two of the conspirators. Shakespeare's company performed an anonymous play about the affair at the Globe Theater in December 1600, but the play was controversial. Edgar I. Fripp quotes a letter from John Chamberlain to Sir Ralph Winwood:

> *The Tragedy of Gowrie*, with all actions and actors, hath been twice represented by the King's Players, with exceeding concourse of all sorts of people; but whether the matter or manner be not well handled, or that it be thought unfit that princes should be played on the stage in their life-time, I hear that some great councillors are much displeased with it, and so it is thought it shall be forbidden' (*Shakespeare: Man and Artist*, vol. 2. London: Oxford University Press, 1938, p. 629)

18 Quoted in G.P.V. Akrigg, ed. *Letters of King James VI & I*. Berkeley: University of California Press, 1984, p. 309.

19 See also G.N. Murphy. 'A Note on Iago's Name.' *Literature and Society*. Ed. Bernice Slote. Lincoln: University of Nebraska Press, 1964, pp. 39–43.

20 ' "Spanish" Othello: The Making of Shakespeare's Moor.' *Shakespeare Survey* 35. Ed. Stanley Wells. Cambridge: Cambridge University Press, 1982, p. 103.

21 The biblical Santiago (Old Spanish: *Santo Iago*), the apostle Saint James, preached widely in Iberia, and though martyred in Judea, his remains were thought to be miraculously transported to and interred in Spain around 44 CE. Roman persecution forced the early Christians to abandon the saint's shrine, and, so the legend goes, the saint's burial place was forgotten until the ninth century, when a shining star and heavenly music led a devout pilgrim to the site. About one hundred years later, Santiago de Compostela, 'Saint James in the field of the stars,' became a favored pilgrimage destination, and by the twelfth century it was the most popular shrine in medieval Europe, rivaling Jerusalem and Rome. Shakespeare's Helena, in *All's Well That Ends Well*, writes that she will make a pilgrimage there (3.4.4).

Another part of the Santiago hagiography, one that connects closely with Shakespeare's *Othello*, is the saint as *Matomoro*, 'moorslayer.' This episode recounts that at the Battle of Clavijo (844 CE) Saint James appeared out of the clouds on a white horse to inspire and lead outnumbered Christians to victory over Muslim moors. The mythic Battle was supposedly the first time the war cry 'Santiago' was intoned by Spanish troops (Marc Simmons. 'Santiago: Reality and Myth.' *Santiago: Saint of Two Worlds*. Albuquerque: University of New Mexico Press, 1991, p. 9). Barbara Everett points out that 'During the very years that we presume *Othello* to have been written, ... London had a ringside seat (even if an oblique one) at a crisis in the affairs of the Spanish Moors,' and she cites James' 'pro-Spanish policy' (p. 104). Iago is, in effect, a 'moor slayer,' but ironically Shakespeare's villain defeats the goodly moor Othello. Shakespeare might have thought of Othello as Essex, subject to an ambitious James.

22 David Harris Willson. *King James VI and I*. New York: Oxford University Press, 1967, p. 40.

23 'God-fathering Prince Henry,' in *The Struggle for the Succession in Late Elizabethan England*. Ed. Jean-Christophe Mayer. Montpellier, France: Astraea Texts, 2004, p. 322.

24 Leeds Barroll. *Anna of Denmark, Queen of England*. Philadelphia: University of Pennsylvania Press, 2001. See Appendix, pp. 162–72.

25 See Peter C. Herman, ' "Best of Poets, Best of Kings": King James VI and I and the Scene of Monarchic Verse,' in Daniel Fischlin and Mark Fortier, eds, *Royal Subjects: Essays on the Writings of James VI and I*, Detroit, MI: Wayne State University Press, 2002, pp. 77ff.

26 ' "Othello", "Lepanto" and the Cyprus Wars.' *Shakespeare Survey* 21.

Ed. Kenneth Muir. Cambridge: Cambridge University Press, 1968, pp. 47–52.

27 William Stirling-Maxwell. *Don John of Austria*. Vol. 2. London: Longmans Green, 1833, p. 22.

28 Neil Rhodes, Jennifer Richards and Joseph Marshall, eds, *King James VI and I: Selected Writings*, Aldershot: Ashgate, 2003, p. 95.

29 Perhaps an ironic dig at James' scholarly reputation and supposed reluctance to enter into a war.

30 See Bruce R. Smith. *Homosexual Desire in Shakespeare's England*. Chicago, IL: University of Chicago Press, 1991, pp. 61–62.

31 See, for example, Murray J. Levith. *Shakespeare's Italian Settings and Plays*. London: Macmillan, 1989, pp. 35–39.

32 John Walter Stoye. *English Travellers Abroad 1604–1667*. New York: Octagon Books, 1968, p. 109.

33 David M. Bergeron. *King James and Letters of Homoerotic Desire*. Iowa City: University of Iowa Press, 1999, p. 37. Abbr. henceforth in text, *Letters*.

34 See poem and prefatory matter, *Selected Writings*, pp. 39–48.

35 *Correspondence of King James VI of Scotland with Sir Robert Cecil and Others in England*. New York: AMS Press, 1968, p. xxi.

36 Ackroyd notes, 'It has been suggested that the relative brevity of the play [*Macbeth*] is an indication of the king's span of attention, but this is unlikely' (p. 442).

Chapter 7

1 New York: Scholars' Facsimiles & Reprints, 1938, p. 282a.

2 For the purposes of my analysis here, I consider only the Italian inner play and not the English frame 'Induction.'

3 See Murray J. Levith. *Shakespeare's Italian Settings and Plays*. London: Macmillan, 1989, pp. 42–43.

4 *Shakespeare*. New York: Basic Books, 2003, p. 107.

Bibliography

Ackroyd, Peter. *Shakespeare: The Biography.* New York: Doubleday, 2005.

Adams, Robert M., ed. *Ben Jonson's Plays and Masques.* New York: Norton, 1979.

Akrigg, G.P.V., ed. *Letters of King James VI & I.* Berkeley: University of California Press, 1984.

Allen, Graham. *Intertextuality.* London: Routledge, 2000.

Anderson, Judith H. *Biographical Truth: The Representation of Historical Persons in Tudor-Stuart Writing.* New Haven, CT: Yale University Press, 1984.

—. 'The Conspiracy of Realism: Impasse and Vision in *King Lear.*' *Studies in Philology* 84 (Winter 1987): 1–23.

Ascham, Roger. *The Scholemaster.* Ed. Edward Arber. London: Constable, 1920.

Athanasius, Saint. *The Life of St. Anthony the Great. The Life of St. Hilarion, and Life of St. Paul the First Hermit.* Willits, CA: Eastern Orthodox Books, 1970. 5–50.

Axton, Marie. *The Queen's Two Bodies: Drama and the Elizabethan Succession.* Studies in History, No. 5. London: Royal Historical Society, 1977.

Bacon, Francis. *The Essays.* Mount Vernon, NY: Peter Pauper Press, n.d.

Barkan, Leonard. 'What Did Shakespeare Read?' *Cambridge Companion to Shakespeare.* Margreta de Grazia and Stanley Wells, eds. Cambridge: Cambridge University Press, 2001. 31–47.

Barroll, Leeds. *Anna of Denmark, Queen of England.* Philadelphia: University of Pennsylvania Press, 2001.

Barthes, Roland. *Image, Music, Text.* Trans. Stephen Heath. New York: Hill and Wang, 1977.

Bate, Jonathan. *Shakespeare and Ovid.* Oxford: Clarendon Press, 1994.

Bergeron, David M. *Royal Family, Royal Lovers: King James of England and Scotland.* Columbia: University of Missouri Press, 1991.

—. *King James and Letters of Homoerotic Desire.* Iowa City: University of Iowa Press, 1999.

Bloom, Harold. *The Anxiety of Influence.* New York: Oxford University Press, 1973.

—. *Ruin the Sacred Truths: Poetry and Belief from the Bible to the Present.* Cambridge, MA: Harvard University Press, 1989.

—. *Shakespeare: The Invention of the Human.* New York: Riverhead, 1998.

Bowers, Fredson, ed. *The Complete Works of Christopher Marlowe.* Vol. 2. Cambridge: Cambridge University Press, 1973.

Bradbrook, M.C. *John Webster: Citizen and Dramatist.* New York: Columbia University Press, 1980.

Brockbank, Philip, ed. *The Arden Shakespeare: Coriolanus.* London: Methuen, 1976.

Brody, Alan. *The English Mummers and Their Plays.* Philadelphia: University of Pennsylvania Press, 1969.

Brooks, Harold, ed. *The Arden Shakespeare: A Midsummer Night's Dream.* London: Methuen, 1979.

—. 'Clarence's Dream.' *Shakespeare Survey* 32 (1979): 145–50.

Brown, John Russell, ed. *The Arden Shakespeare: The Merchant of Venice.* New York: Random House, 1964.

Bruce, John. *Correspondence of King James VI of Scotland with Sir Robert Cecil and Others in England.* New York: AMS Press, 1968.

Bullen, A.H., ed. *The Works of John Marston.* Vol. 3. London: John C. Nimmo, 1887.

Bullough, Geoffrey, ed. *Narrative and Dramatic Sources of Shakespeare.* 8 vols. London: Routledge and Kegan Paul, 1957–75.

Campbell, Joseph. *The Hero with a Thousand Faces.* Cleveland, OH: Meridian Books, 1956.

Caxton, William, trans. of Jacobus de Voraigne. *The Golden Legend or Lives of the Saints.* 7 vols. London: J.M. Dent, 1900. 125–34.

Chambers, E.K. *William Shakespeare: A Study of Facts and Problems.* 2 vols. Oxford: Clarendon Press, 1930.

Clemen, Wolfgang. *The Development of Shakespeare's Imagery.* New York: Hill and Wang, 1951.

Cox-Rearick, Janet, ed. *Giulio Romano: Master Designer.* New York: Hunter College, 1999.

Craik, T.W., ed. *The Oxford Shakespeare: The Merry Wives of Windsor.* Oxford: Clarendon Press, 1989.

Crane, R.S. 'The Vogue of *Guy of Warwick* From the Close of the Middle Ages to the Romantic Revival.' *PMLA* 30 (1915): 125–94.

Creizenach, Wilhelm. *The English Drama in the Age of Shakespeare.* Philadelphia, PA: Lippincott, 1916.

Cust, Lionel and Mary F.S. Hervey. 'The Lumley Inventories' and 'A Lumley Inventory of 1609.' Vol. 6. Oxford: Walpole Society, 1918. 15–50.

Eliot, T.S. *Essays on Elizabethan Drama.* New York: Harcourt, Brace, and World (Harvest), 1956.

—. *The Sacred Wood: Essays on Poetry and Criticism.* New York: University Paperbacks, 1960.

Evans, G. Blackmore, Herschel Baker, Anne Barton, Frank Kermode, Harry Levin, Hallett Smith and Marie Edel, eds. *The Riverside Shakespeare.* Second ed. Houghton Mifflin, 1997.

Everett, Barbara. ' "Spanish" Othello: The Making of Shakespeare's Moor.' *Shakespeare Survey* 35. Ed. Stanley Wells. Cambridge: Cambridge University Press, 1982: 101–12.

Fehl, Philipp. 'Realism and Classicism in the Representation of a Painful Scene: Titian's "Flaying of Marsyas" in the Archiepiscopal Palace at Kromeriz.' *Czechoslovakia Past and Present.* Vol. 2. Ed. Miloslav Rechcigl, Jr. The Hague: Mouton, 1968. 1387–415.

Ferguson, George. *Signs and Symbols in Christian Art.* New York: Oxford University Press, 1961.

Foucault, Michel. 'What is an Author?' *The Book History Reader.* David Finkelstein and Alistair McCleery, eds. London: Routledge, 2002. 225–30.

Freake, Douglas. '*A Midsummer Night's Dream* as a Comic version of the Theseus Myth.' *A Midsummer Night's Dream: Critical Essays.* Ed. Dorothea Kehler. New York: Garland, 1998. 259–74.

Freedberg, Sydney J. 'Titian and Marsyas.' *FMR* 4 (1984). 51–64.

Fripp, Edgar I. *Shakespeare: Man and Artist.* Vol. 2. London: Oxford University Press, 1938.

Geneva Bible: A Facsimile of the 1560 Edition. Madison: University of Wisconsin Press, 1969.

Gillespie, Stuart. *Shakespeare's Books: A Dictionary of Shakespeare's Sources.* London: Athlone, 2001.

Graves, Robert. *The Greek Myths.* Vol. 2. Harmondsworth: Penguin, 1955.

Greenblatt, Stephen, Walter Cohen, Jean E. Howard and Katharine Eisaman Maus, eds. *The Norton Shakespeare.* New York: Norton, 1997.

Greenlaw, Edward, Charles G. Osgood and Frederick H. Padelford. *The Works of Edmund Spenser.* Vol. 1. Baltimore, MD: The Johns Hopkins University Press, 1932.

Halio, Jay L., ed. *The Oxford Shakespeare: The Merchant of Venice.* Oxford: Clarendon Press, 1993.

Hamilton, A.C. et al., eds. *The Spenser Encyclopedia.* Toronto: University of Toronto Press, 1990.

Hammond, Anthony, ed. *The Arden Shakespeare: King Richard III.* London: Methuen, 1981.

Harbage, Alfred. 'A Contemporary Attack on Shakespeare.' *Shakespeare Association Bulletin* 16 (1941): 42–49.

Hartt, Frederick. *Giulio Romano.* Vol. 2. New Haven, CT: Yale University Press, 1958.

Herman, Peter C. ' "Best of Poets, Best of Kings": King James VI and I and the Scene of Monarchic Verse.' *Royal Subjects: Essays on the Writings of James VI and I.* Daniel Fischlin and Mark Fortier, eds. Detroit, MI: Wayne State University Press, 2002. 75–101.

Hervey, Mary F.S. *The Life and Correspondence of Thomas Howard, Earl of Arundel.* Cambridge: Cambridge University Press, 1921.

Hieatt, A. Kent. 'William Shakespeare.' *The Spenser Encyclopedia.* A.C. Hamilton, Donald Cheney, W.F. Blissett, David A. Richardson and William W. Barker, eds. Toronto: University of Toronto Press, 1990. 641.

Hillman, Richard. 'God-fathering Prince Henry.' *The Struggle for the Succession in Late Elizabethan England.* Ed. Jean-Christophe Mayer. Montpellier, France: Astraea Texts, 2004. 313–26.

Holland, Peter. 'Theseus's Shadows in *A Midsummer Night's Dream.*' *Shakespeare and the Literary Tradition.* Eds Stephen Orgel and Sean Keilen. New York: Garland, 1999. 139-151.

Honigmann, E.A.J., ed. *The Arden Shakespeare: Othello.* Third ed. Walton-on-Thames: Thomas Nelson, 1997.

Horwich, Richard. 'Riddle and Dilemma in *The Merchant of Venice.*' *Studies in English Literature* 17 (1977): 191–200.

Howarth, David. *Lord Arundel and His Circle.* New Haven, CT: Yale University Press, 1985.

Hunter, G.K. *John Lyly: The Humanist as Courtier.* Cambridge, MA: Harvard University Press, 1962.

—. 'The Theology of Marlowe's *The Jew of Malta.*' *Journal of the Warburg and Courtauld Institute* 27 (1964): 211–40.

Johnson, Richard. *The Seven Champions of Christendom (1596/97).* Ed. Jennifer Fellows. Aldershot: Ashgate, 2003.

Jones, Emrys. ' "Othello", "Lepanto" and the Cyprus Wars.' *Shakespeare Survey* 21. Ed. Kenneth Muir. Cambridge: Cambridge University Press, 1968: 47–52.

Jones, John Henry, ed. *The English Faust Book.* Cambridge: Cambridge University Press, 1994.

Jorgens, Jack J. *Shakespeare on Film.* Bloomington: University of Indiana Press, 1977.

Jump, John D., ed. *The Revels Plays: Doctor Faustus by Christopher Marlowe.* London: Methuen, 1962.

Kendall, Paul Murray. *Richard the Third.* New York: Norton, 1956.

Knight, G. Wilson. *The Sovereign Flower.* London: Methuen, 1958.

Kott, Jan. *Shakespeare Our Contemporary.* Trans. Boleslaw Taborski. Garden City, NY: Anchor Books, 1966.

—. *The Bottom Translation: Marlowe and Shakespeare and the Carnival Tradition.* Trans. Daniela Miedzyrzecka and Lillian Vallee. Evanston, IL: Northwestern University Press, 1987.

Kristeva, Julia. *Séméotikè: Recherches pour une sémanalyse.* Paris: Editions du Seuil, 1969.

Lamb, M.E. '*A Midsummer-Night's Dream:* The Myth of Theseus and the Minotaur.' *Texas Studies in Literature and Language* 21:4 (Winter 1979): 478–91.

Laroque, François. 'An Analogue and Possible Secondary Source to the Pound-of-Flesh Story in *The Merchant of Venice.*' *Notes and Queries* (New Series) 30 (April 1983): 117–18.

Levith, Murray J. *What's in Shakespeare's Names.* Hamden, CT: Archon, 1978.

—. *Shakespeare's Italian Settings and Plays.* London: Macmillan, 1989.

Lewalski, Barbara. 'Biblical Allusion and Allegory in *The Merchant of Venice.*' *Shakespeare Quarterly* 13 (1962): 327–43.

Lewis, Cynthia. *Particular Saints: Shakespeare's Four Antonios, Their Contexts, and Their Plays.* Newark: University of Delaware Press, 1997.

Lisak, Catherine. ' "Succession" versus "Usurpation": Politics and Rhetoric in Shakespeare's *Richard II.*' *The Struggle for the Succession in Late Elizabethan England: Politics, Polemics and Cultural Representation.* Ed. Jean-Christophe Mayer. Montpellier, France: Astraea Texts, 2004. 353–70.

Lynch, Stephen J. *Shakespearean Intertextuality: Studies in Selected Sources and Plays.* Westport, CT: Greenwood Press, 1998.

Marlowe, Christopher. *Doctor Faustus.* Ed. Sylvan Barnet. New York: New American Library, 1969.

Mayer, Jean-Christophe, ed. *Breaking the Silence on the Succession.* Montpellier, France: Astraea Texts, 2003.

MacLachlan, Hugh. 'St. George.' *The Spenser Encyclopedia.* Eds A.C. Hamilton, Donald Cheney, W.F. Blissett, David A. Richardson and William W. Barker. Toronto: University of Toronto Press, 1990. 329–30.

Melchiori, Giorgio, ed. *The Arden Shakespeare: The Merry Wives of Windsor.* Third ed. Walton-on-Thames: Thomas Nelson, 2000.

Meres, Francis. *Palladis Tamia: Wit's Treasury.* New York: Scholars' Facsimiles & Reprints, 1938.

Michie, James. Trans. *Ovid: The Art of Love.* New York: Modern Library, 2002.

Miola, Robert S. *Shakespeare's Reading.* Oxford: Oxford University Press, 2000.

Mowat, Barbara A. ' "A local habitation and a name": Shakespeare's Text as Construct.' *Style* 23:3 (Fall 1989): 336.

Muir, Kenneth. *Sources of Shakespeare's Plays.* New Haven, CT: Yale University Press, 1977.

Murphy, G.N. 'A Note on Iago's Name.' *Literature and Society.* Ed. Bernice Slote. Lincoln: University of Nebraska Press, 1964. 39–43.

Murray, John Tucker. *English Dramatic Companies 1558–1642.* 2 vols. New York: Russell and Russell, 1963.

Nagle, Betty Rose, trans. *Ovid's Fasti: Roman Holidays.* Bloomington: Indiana University Press, 1995.

Neumann, Jaromir. *Titian: The Flaying of Marsyas.* Trans. Till Gottheimer. London: Spring Books, 1962.

Nigg, Joseph, ed. *The Book of Fabulous Beasts.* New York: Oxford University Press, 1999.

Nims, John Frederick, ed. *Ovid's Metamorphoses: The Arthur Golding Translation 1567.* Philadelphia, PA: Paul Dry Books, 2000.

North, Thomas, trans. *Plutarch's The Lives of the Noble Grecians and Romans.* Vol. 1. New York: Heritage Press, 1941.

Orgel, Stephen. *The Authentic Shakespeare.* New York: Routledge, 2002.

Ormerod, David. '*A Midsummer Night's Dream:* The Monster in the Labyrinth.' *Shakespeare Studies* 11 (1978): 39–52.

Pafford, J.H.P. *The Arden Shakespeare: The Winter's Tale.* London: Methuen, 1963.

Parker, Barbara L. *Plato's Republic and Shakespeare's Rome: A Political Study of the Roman Works.* Newark: University of Delaware Press, 2004.

Pearson, D'Orsay. ' "Unkinde" Theseus: A Study in Renaissance Mythography.' *English Literary Renaissance* 4:2 (Spring 1974): 276–98.

Phillips, James Emerson. *Images of a Queen: Mary Stuart in Sixteenth-Century Literature.* Berkeley: University of California Press, 1964.

Plottel, Jeanine Parisier. 'Introduction,' *Intertextuality: New Perspectives in Criticism. New York Literary Forum.* Vol. 2. Eds. Jeanine Parisier Plottel and Hanna Charney, 1978. xi–xx.

Potts, Abbie Findlay. *Shakespeare and The Faerie Queene.* Ithaca, NY: Cornell University Press, 1958.

Purcell, Mary. *St. Anthony and His Times.* Dublin: M.H. Gill, 1960.

Rackham, H., trans. *Pliny: Natural History.* Cambridge, MA: Harvard University Press, 1956.

Rhodes, Neil, Jennifer Richards and Joseph Marshall, eds. *King James VI and I: Selected Writings.* Aldershot: Ashgate, 2003.

Ridley, M.R., ed. *The Arden Shakespeare: Othello.* New York: Vintage, 1967.

Roberts, Jeanne Addison. *Shakespeare's English Comedy.* Lincoln: University of Nebraska Press, 1979.

Robinson, F.N., ed. *The Works of Geoffrey Chaucer.* Boston, MA: Houghton-Mifflin, 1957.

Rosenberg, Pierre. 'The Flaying of Marsyas.' In *Titian: Prince of Painters.* Eds. Susanne Biadene and Mary Yakush. New York: Prestel, 1990. 370–72.

Rouse, W.H.D., ed. *Shakespeare's Ovid: Being Arthur Golding's Translation of the Metamorphoses.* Carbondale: Southern Illinois University Press, 1961.

Sandys, George. *Ovid's Metamorphosis Englished, Mythologized, and Represented in Figures.* Karl K. Hulley and Stanley T. Vandersall, eds. Lincoln: University of Nebraska Press, 1970.

Shapiro, James. *Shakespeare and the Jews.* New York: Columbia University Press, 1996.

—. *A Year in the Life of William Shakespeare, 1599.* New York: Harper Collins, 2005.

Shattuck, Roger. *Forbidden Knowledge.* New York: St. Martin's, 1996.

Siegel, Paul. 'Shylock and the Puritan Usurers.' *Studies in Shakespeare.* Arthur D. Matthews and Clark M. Emery, eds. Coral Gables, FL: University of Miami Press, 1953. 129–38.

—. 'Shylock the Puritan.' *Columbia University Forum* 5 (Fall 1962): 14–19.

Simmons, Marc. 'Santiago: Reality and Myth.' *Santiago: Saint of Two Worlds.* Albuquerque: University of New Mexico Press, 1991.

Smith, Bruce R. *Homosexual Desire in Shakespeare's England.* Chicago, IL: University of Chicago Press, 1991.

Spurgeon, Caroline. *Shakespeare's Imagery.* New York: Macmillan, 1935.

Steadman, John M. 'Falstaff as Actaeon: A Dramatic Emblem.' *Shakespeare Quarterly* 14:3 (Summer 1963): 231–44.

Stirling-Maxwell, William. *Don John of Austria.* Vol. 2. London: Longmans Green, 1833.

Stoye, John Walter. *English Travellers Abroad 1604–1667.* New York: Octagon Books, 1968.

Tillyard, E.M.W. *Shakespeare's History Plays.* New York: Collier Books, 1962.

Verheyen, Egon. *The Palazzo del Te in Mantua: Images of Love and Politics.* Baltimore, MD: The Johns Hopkins University Press, 1977.

Watkins, W.B.C. *Shakespeare and Spenser.* Princeton, NJ: Princeton University Press, 1950.

Wethey, Harold E. *Titian.* 3 vols. London: Phaidon, 1975.

White, T.H., ed. *The Book of Beasts.* London: Jonathan Cape, 1954.

Whitworth, Charles. 'Thomas Lodge: *The Wounds of Civil War* and the Elizabethan Succession Crisis.' *The Struggle for the Succession in Late Elizabethan England.* Ed. Jean-Christophe Mayer. Montpellier, France: Astraea Texts, 2004. 299–311.

Willson, David Harris. *King James VI and I.* New York: Oxford University Press, 1967.

Wilson, F.P. *The English Drama 1485–1585.* New York: Oxford University Press, 1969.

Withycombe, E.G. *The Oxford Dictionary of English Christian Names.* London: Oxford University Press, 1973.

Wood, Michael. *Shakespeare.* New York: Basic Books, 2003.

Worden, Blair. 'Which Play was Performed at the Globe Theatre on 7 February 1601?' *London Review of Books* 25:13 (July 10, 2003): 22–24.

Yates, Frances A. *The Occult Philosophy in the Elizabethan Age.* London: Ark Paperbacks, 1983.

Index: Shakespeare's Cues and Prompts